**Bilingual/
Bicultural
Education
And
Teacher
Training**

Bilingual/ Bicultural Education And Teacher Training

National Education Association
Washington, D.C.

by
Henry J. Casso

Published in cooperation with
the ERIC Clearinghouse on Teacher Education

Stock No. 1602-5-00 (paper)
            1607-6-00 (cloth)

Note

The opinions expressed in this publication should not be construed as representing the policy or position of the National Education Association. Materials published as part of NEA's Professional Studies series are intended to be discussion documents for teachers who are concerned with specialized interests of the profession.

Library of Congress Cataloging in Publication Data

Casso, Henry J
    Bilingual/bicultural education and teacher training.

    (Professional studies)
    Bibliography: p.
    1. Education, Bilingual—United States. 2. Teachers,
Training of—United States. I. Title. II. Series.
LC3731.C35   371.9'7   76-45392
    ISBN 0-8106-1602-5

CONTENTS

CONTENTS (Continued)

I. THE RENAISSANCE IN BILINGUAL/BICULTURAL EDUCATION

Bilingual/bicultural education in the United States is undergoing a renaissance, one of the most important, dynamic, and dramatic reform movements in the history of American public education. The renaissance comes at a time when the country is celebrating its Bicentennial, when the interdependence of nations has become an imperative, when larger nations are increasingly dependent on smaller ones for basic natural resources, when our country has welcomed Vietnamese refugees. It has serious implications for minorities (linguistically and culturally distinct students), for the majority (monolingual students), for present and future teachers, and for those educational entities responsible for preservice and in-service teacher training.

The bilingual/bicultural education movement is offering hope to hundreds of thousands of linguistically and culturally distinct peoples of the United States. It has been argued that the traditional system has benefited linguistically and culturally distinct students, but it is more commonly accepted that the public schools have benefited chiefly those students who reflect the ideal monolingual/monocultural model. We are beginning to realize that the American public educational experience has not proved to be as beneficial as it could have been[1] or as it needs to be to strengthen our society. Bilingual/bicultural education reform offers new opportunities to that society and to linguistically and culturally distinct students.

In considering the importance of this educational reform, we cannot discount current opinion that the essential role of public education is the development of a responsive citizenry for the twenty-first century. The bilingual/bicultural education renaissance is important because it is founded on notions of (a) equality of educational opportunity and (b) accountability in public education. The notions of equal educational opportunity and accountability have had a significant impact on the growth of bilingual/bicultural education; and it must be added that bilingual/bicultural education is a direct response to current public admission of the failure of public schools to educate children.[2]

The dynamics of bilingual/bicultural education reform are such that in less than 10 years a drastic change has occurred in the United States. There has been a strong movement away from the traditional monolingual education laws, policies, attitudes, and practices of most school systems. Formerly, practically all the states of the Union had some legislation or official policy publicly excluding formal instruction in any language other than English. Today only six states (Delaware, Iowa, Minnesota, North Carolina, Rhode Island, and West Virginia) maintain a law or policy against the use of a language other than English for instruction. On the other hand, according to a study prepared for the National Bilingual Bicultural Institute held in Tucson in 1973,[3] 15 states had a policy favoring bilingual/bicultural education.

To give a federal perspective, it should be noted that the first national Bilingual Education Act, passed in 1968, also known as Title VII of the Elementary and Secondary Education Act (ESEA), had a first-year funding of $7.5 million. By 1974, Title VII was funded at $58.35 million. In FY 1975 this was increased to $85 million. In 1969, there were more than one hundred bilingual education projects under Title VII; by 1974-75 the number had risen to 328. While the key language of these programs is Spanish, there are also programs in 23 Native

American languages, 11 Pacific and Asian languages, and 8 European languages. The 1974 Education Amendments provided for increased involvement at the higher education level. (See Appendixes A and B.)

The bilingual/bicultural education movement also received support through the Voter Registration Act of 1975. That law addresses for the first time linguistically and culturally distinct communities other than Blacks, for whom the original act was intended. The law was expanded to provide for the unique linguistic needs and characteristics of the Spanish-speaking (the majority of whom are Mexican Americans), and of Native Americans, Alaskans, and Asian Americans.

The significance of the 1975 Voter Registration Act was noted in an article in *U.S. News and World Report*. Whereas the former law concerned itself with Blacks in "six Southern States—Alabama, Georgia, Louisiana, Mississippi, Virginia and South Carolina—and ... small portions of Hawaii, Arizona, California, Connecticut, Idaho, New Hampshire, New York, Maine, Massachusetts and Wyoming ... added under the new Act will be areas with concentrations of 'language minorities' where election material has been printed only in English and where the turnout for the 1972 election fell below half the voting-age residents, or where illiteracy in English is high."[4] Sixteen additional states—Alaska, Colorado, Florida, Kansas, Minnesota, Montana, Nebraska, Nevada, New Mexico, North Dakota, Oklahoma, Oregon, South Dakota, Texas, Utah, and Washington—will be affected because of the "linguistic needs of the citizens." This event has far-reaching implications for society in general and educators in particular.

The bilingual/bicultural education movement is dramatic in that, whereas historically it has been perceived as socially and educationally disadvantageous to speak a language other than English, presently it is esteemed educationally and economically advantageous to do so. Although we will examine some of the causes for this growth later, it is well to note here that some of the impetus is due to the moving of international companies into Latin America, the growth of multinational companies, and the shift of the oil monopoly to the Middle East. Without a doubt, success for the merchant, lawyer, engineer, architect, educator, financier, economist, communicator, and government representative in these new societal, international dynamics depends on familiarity with the culture and language of another country. It is certainly a different and new era. Interestingly enough, one of the four most frequently spoken and internationally recognized languages is the language of the majority of the 210 million people in nations that are the Southern neighbors of the United States—Spanish.

What are some of the reasons why only now in the United States, after 200 years, there exists an atmosphere where this dramatic surge can take place? What are some of the events and circumstances which led to this renaissance? Certainly these are common questions which arise with teachers, counselors, administrators, and other school people around the country. They are asked in newspaper editorials in communities where bilingual/bicultural education programs have been attempted, have begun, or flourish.

The renaissance of bilingual/bicultural education had several different starting points. A number of parallel national and regional events took place in the 1960's which provided the atmosphere for the revival. It is not the purpose of this study to conjecture which of these events contributed most to the growth of bilingual/

bicultural education. It is sufficient to identify some of the significant historical landmarks. These are not given in chronological order because we are too close in history to these events to make a judgment about which event did what.

HUMAN RIGHTS AND THE SURGE FOR SELF-DETERMINATION

The sixties were greatly affected by the civil rights movement, pushed especially by the Black communities. During this same period, Chicano and Puerto Rican youth were manifesting their concerns particularly in the quest for improved education. In the Chicano student walkouts in more than a dozen communities—urban and rural, large and small—one of the issues promoted was bilingual/bicultural education.[5]

In the surge for self-determination, the schools were a focus of attention since they were seen as pivotal to the development of leadership in each community. There was a reassessment of the value of schooling and education by both the communities and school officials. As the various linguistically and culturally distinct communities scrutinized the schools, it became clear that both communities and families were excluded from positive self-identification in such critical areas as textbooks, curriculum, and history. There was a surge for self-identification and formation of a positive self-image in history, culture, and language through the school.

The bilingual/bicultural education movement was seen first by community leadership, then by parents and students, as the means of fostering a positive self-image.

THE IMPACT OF U. S. INVOLVEMENT IN WARS

It has been well-documented that military service during World War II enabled many to seek further education under the G.I. Bill, whether it was completion of high school or pursuit of postsecondary education. Service in the Korean and Vietnamese wars also enabled young men and women to seek further education. A new ingredient was emerging: pride of self and a desire to know more about one's language and culture.

THE GROWTH OF THE EQUAL OPPORTUNITY MOVEMENT

The dramatic push in the mid-sixties for equal rights was logically and quickly extended to include equal educational opportunity, specific meanings and applications of which have been the topic of much debate among educators. For our purposes, the very notion of equal educational opportunity is the criterion which helps us assess the caliber of education for Chicano and other linguistically and culturally distinct children.

The notion of bilingual education is not new in the United States, but the significant feature of the renaissance is the association of bilingual education with the ideas of fundamental rights and equal educational opportunity. This, as will be seen later, has enabled the courts and state legislatures to move bilingual/bicultural education as an educational program much more rapidly.

ACCOUNTABILITY IN PUBLIC EDUCATION

The push for and growth of equal educational opportunity at national, regional, state, and local levels have provided fertile ground for the growth of the notion of accountability. This notion, too, means many things to many educators. For our purposes, the significant transition of just a few years ago from merely equalizing facilities to measuring educational inputs against outcomes,[6] and now to holding teachers and school administrators responsible for outcomes, forces school officials to seek solutions for the more and more identifiable areas of failure, especially for the great numbers of linguistically and culturally distinct students.

> In one major Southwestern city, the Office for Civil Rights found that the initial assignment of educational materials and the determination of educational level, that is, the level of the textbook series, was made on a school-by-school basis, without any attempt to measure the educational potential or achievement of the individual children in the school. All of the children in the schools in the district, with a predominant enrollment of minority children (Blacks and Mexican Americans), were assigned textbooks at the remedial and low-average levels. [7]

In a word, the practices of yesteryear—of allowing students to repeat grades without end, to be placed indiscriminately in educable mentally retarded (EMR) classes far beyond the percentage of population of their respective communities, to be pushed out of school, and the many other practices which were taken for granted—would no longer be tolerated under this new notion. What was the solution? What could be done about it? What was the alternative?

Bilingual/bicultural education was being offered as an alternative educational strategy to what had preceded, which had produced the awesome statistic of low educational achievement of children/students whose language and culture were not those of the school.

THE CUBAN REFUGEE PROGRAM

With the massive exodus of Cuban citizens to Miami after the Castro revolution in 1959, Florida's public school system was suddenly faced with having to provide education for thousands of immigrant children. As teachers and professors were among the professional groups forced to leave Cuba, the Florida schools had access to teachers in the language and culture of the new students. The schools had been accustomed to a monolingual/monocultural process of instruction in English, but the Cubans brought a new culture and language. The dilemma was, should the children and teachers first learn English, or should bilingual education (education in both languages) be given a chance? Fortunately, the latter method was chosen, and this event was to have significant influence in promoting the current acceptance and growth of bilingual education in the United States.

MAJOR EDUCATIONAL STUDIES AND PUBLIC HEARINGS

The early part of the 1960's saw the beginning of a concerted effort to provide more accurate data on the outcomes of public education, especially as related to linguistically and culturally distinct children/students in general and Mexican American children/students in particular. It was significant that such efforts were undertaken by both nongovernmental organizations and government agencies. Each type contributed to the growth of bilingual/bicultural education.

Nongovernmental Efforts

The best and most important nongovernmental efforts in behalf of linguistically and culturally distinct students were those of the National Education Association (NEA). The force of the largest teacher organization in the United States could hardly be ignored.

The NEA's position was stated in a report entitled *The Invisible Minority*:

> The most acute educational problem in [the elementary and secondary schools of] the Southwest is that which involves Mexican-American children . . . . Many of these young people experience academic failure in school. At best, they have limited success. A large percentage become school dropouts.[8]

In setting up the investigating team of teachers who were to produce this report, the NEA realized that there were some teachers who were individually initiating efforts to do something about the reported "failure." Two early positions which motivated the decision-makers and teachers of the NEA to conduct an investigation were (a) to help Mexican American students adjust to the dominant Anglo culture, and (b) to foster in them a pride in their Spanish-speaking culture and Mexican origin.[9]

Important for our purposes in understanding the current growth of bilingual/bicultural education is the fact that the NEA, a teacher association, publicly admitted something known by teachers and many parents but neither acknowledged nor practiced by educators:

> . . . that Spanish properly used can be a bridge to the learning of English instead of an obstacle and that Mexican-American students can become truly bilingual and bicultural.[10]

The body of the report gives a brief description of 357 years of history, describes how a majority became a minority, relates the legacy of poverty, addresses the low-achiever and drop-out issues, questions whether something was inherently wrong with the public school system of instruction, identifies barriers to and bastions of learning, recognizes that many states prohibited teaching in any language other than English, and even recognizes that there were too many instances in which official school policies prohibited the speaking of Spanish on school grounds. The report addresses the stereotype issue and, finally, looks at the student's damaged self-image brought about by the educational process.

Central to the report are the general recommendations the task force made after visiting a number of bilingual projects and establishing the negative outcomes of the public schools of the Southwest. Keep in mind that the recommendations were made as early as 1965-66. Ten years have now passed, and some of them have direct application today.

Before identifying the recommendations, it is worth mentioning that the report sets aside a specific chapter on teacher selection and preparation, a topic we will take up later (in Part III). Although the report probably has been a source of influence on the development of national legislation, it is interesting to observe that higher education institutions have not given proper attention to its suggestions in the area of teacher training.

The specific recommendations on bilingual education are as follows:

1. Instruction in pre-school and throughout the early grades should be in both Spanish and English.
2. English should be taught as a second language.
3. Contemporaneously there should be emphasis on the reading, writing, and speaking of good Spanish, since Mexican-American children are so often illiterate in it.
4. A well-articulated program of instruction in the mother tongue should be continued from pre-school through the high school years.
5. All possible measures should be taken to help Mexican-American children gain a pride in their ancestral culture and language.
6. Schools should recruit Spanish-speaking teachers and teachers' aides . . . .
7. Schools, colleges, and universities should conduct research in bilingual education, train or retrain bilingual teachers, create appropriate materials and, in general, establish a strong tradition of bilingual education . . . .
8. School districts desiring to develop good bilingual programs but lacking funds should look to the possibility of financing them under new federal programs and in some cases state compensatory education programs.
9. State laws which specify English as the language of instruction and thus, by implication at least, outlaw the speaking of Spanish except in Spanish classes should be repealed.[11]

Since it was this report that occasioned a symposium on "The Spanish-Speaking Child in the Schools of the Southwest" at the University of Arizona in Tucson, wherein this report was the highlight of discussion, it can reasonably be concluded that the committee, the report, and the NEA can be credited for much that resulted from that symposium. Participating were a number of educators, leaders, and politicians from around the United States who later were to take significant roles in their respective states and institutions.[12] Three of those who were actively involved in the Tucson conference later were key persons in the development of the first national bilingual education legislation: Senator Joseph Montoya of New Mexico and Senator Ralph Yarborough of Texas, who were members of the Committee on Labor and Public Welfare; and Monroe Sweetland of the NEA.

Government Efforts

Forerunners of and important governmental contributors to the atmosphere promoting the renaissance of bilingual/bicultural education include the U.S. Commission on Civil Rights, the U.S. Senate Subcommittee on Bilingual Education, and the Senate Subcommittee on Equal Educational Opportunity. The Office for Civil Rights of the U.S. Department of Health, Education, and Welfare (OCR/HEW) also played a significant role, as described in the next section on major court action.

The U.S. Commission on Civil Rights. This Commission was established by Congress to provide hearings, studies, data, and recommendations on the rights of U.S. citizens and areas where these rights may have been infringed upon. In 1968 the Commission began what was to become the most exhaustive educational research on Mexican Americans in U.S. history.

The Commission reviewed the educational outcomes of the Southwestern schools, introducing a significant first. Whereas many educational researchers formerly measured the success or equality of public education by the "inputs," the Commission's assessment of the Southwestern schools was based on five measurable areas of "outcomes":

1. The holding power of the schools, or the drop-out factor
2. Grade repetition
3. Reading levels
4. Overageness in classes
5. Percentage of students entering postsecondary education.

These findings were published in a series of Mexican American Education Study reports, as follows:

Ethnic Isolation of Mexican Americans in the Public Schools of the Southwest (Report I). This report examines the extent to which Chicanos are segregated in the schools of the Southwest as well as the underrepresentation of Mexican Americans as teachers.

The Unfinished Education: Outcomes for Minorities in the Five Southwestern States (Report II). This report documents the failure of schools to educate Mexican Americans and other minority students as measured in terms of reading achievement, school holding power, grade repetition, overageness, and participation in extracurricular activities.

The Excluded Student: Educational Practices Affecting Mexican Americans in the Southwest (Report III). This report describes the exclusionary practices of schools in dealing with the unique linguistic and cultural characteristics of Chicano students.

Mexican American Education in Texas: A Function of Wealth (Report IV). This report examines the ways in which the Texas school finance system works to the detriment of districts in which Mexican American students are concentrated.

Teachers and Students: Differences in Teacher Interaction with Mexican American and Anglo Students (Report V). This report focuses on teacher-pupil verbal behavior in the classroom, measuring the extent to which differences exist in the verbal interactions of teachers toward their Chicano and their Anglo pupils.

Toward Quality Education for Mexican Americans (Report VI). This report contains summary, conclusions, and recommendations.

There is a close parallel between the last of the Commission's reports and the NEA report, since both make major recommendations based on investigative findings. The Commission's recommendations do consider other vital educational areas such as curriculum, student assignment, counseling, and Title VI of the Civil Rights Act. The major conclusions of the Commission were as follows:

> Entrance into public school brings about an abrupt change for all children, but for many Mexican American children the change is often shattering. The knowledge and skills they have gained in their early years are regarded as valueless in the world of the schools. The language which most Chicano children have learned—Spanish—is not the language of the school and is either ignored or actively suppressed. Even when the Spanish language is deemed an acceptable medium of communication by the schools, the Chicano's particular dialect is often considered "substandard" or no language at all . . . with little or no assistance, Mexican American children are expected to master this language [English] while competing on equal terms with their Anglo classmates.
>
> The curriculum which the schools offer seldom includes items of particular relevance to Chicano children and often damages the perception which Chicanos have gained of their culture and heritage. It is a curriculum developed by agencies and institutions from which Mexican Americans are almost entirely excluded.
>
> Chicano children also are taught primarily by teachers who are Anglo. Generally, these teachers are uninformed on the culture that Chicanos bring to school and unfamiliar with the language they speak. The teachers themselves have been trained at institutions staffed almost entirely by Anglos, and their training and practice teaching do little to develop in them the skills necessary to teach Mexican American children.[13]

The Commission urged that "state legislatures . . . enact legislation requiring districts to establish bilingual education or other curricular approaches designed to impart English language skills to non-English-speaking students . . . ." It urged Congress to "increase its support for bilingual education," and recommended that the National Institute of Education (NIE) "fund research to develop curricular programs designed to meet the educational needs of Chicano students."[14]

Specifically in the area of teacher education, the Commission made the following recommendations:

1. Teacher education institutions in the Southwest should incorporate information about Chicanos in each of their foundation courses . . . . These courses should develop in all trainees:

   (a) An understanding and appreciation of the history, language, culture, and individual differences of Chicanos.

    (b) The ability to facilitate the fullest possible development of Chicano students' potential.

    (c) Skill in interacting positively with Chicano students and adults.

2. Teacher education institutions in the Southwest should assure that trainees perform a portion of their practice teaching in schools with Chicano students, and under the supervision of teachers and professors who have demonstrated skill in teaching Chicano as well as Anglo students . . . .

6. School districts in the Southwest should update the teaching skills of present instructional staff by providing in-service training that incorporates the elements specified in recommendations 1 and 2 . . . .

8. State departments of education should establish procedures to assess the language skills and cultural understanding of applicants for teaching certificates and should indicate on all certificates which linguistically and culturally different groups of students the certificate holder is qualifed to teach.

9. State departments of education should issue requirements that districts with students whose primary language is not English must provide teachers who speak the students' language and understand their cultural background.[15]

The Commission's interest and support and its recommendation of bilingual/bicultural education as a viable strategy to provide equal educational opportunity for the linguistically and culturally distinct child moved it to develop a further document dedicated completely to the question of bilingual/bicultural education, released in May 1975—*A Better Chance To Learn: Bilingual Bicultural Education.*

This work, which took more than a year to develop, was extremely timely since it followed the Supreme Court decision in *Lau v. Nichols* and the subsequent establishment of 10 regional Lau centers (see Appendix C) designated to assist school districts, state departments of education, and teacher training institutions in the area of quality education programs for the linguistically and culturally distinct child.

A Better Chance To Learn is an important additional contribution of the Civil Rights Commission to the renaissance of bilingual/bicultural education. The report falls short, however, of providing enough developmental background for legal perspectives on bilingual/bicultural notions today. It leans heavily on the language portion alone, only alluding to the cultural aspect of bilingual/bicultural education. The report concluded:

> The Commission's basic conclusion is that bilingual bicultural education is the program of instruction which currently offers the best vehicle for large numbers of language minority students who experience language difficulty in our schools.[16]

Beyond the educational benefits of bilingual/bicultural programs which the report outlined earlier, these benefits were noted:

> Teachers are included who bring the native language and culture to the educational program . . . . The native culture is integrated into the curriculum, so

that the historical, literary, and political contributions of members of language minority groups to this country are included in educational course matter. Finally, bilingual bicultural programs encourage the involvement of language minority parents and community persons in school activities.[17]

Hearings and Hearings Reports. Various public hearings have contributed greatly to the current thrust of bilingual/bicultural education, providing important data for national or statewide legislation, appropriations, or policy. Such hearings have been held by congressional subcommittees and the U.S. Commission on Civil Rights. The student, teacher, or teacher educator in bilingual/bicultural education is seldom made aware of the information derived from these sessions. This section will deal with hearings of (a) the U.S. Senate Special Subcommittee on Bilingual Education, (b) the U.S. Senate Subcommittee on Equal Educational Opportunity, and (c) the U.S. Commission on Civil Rights (national and statewide hearings).

(a) *U.S. Senate Special Subcommittee on Bilingual Education.* Following the NEA-Tucson conference, and greatly influenced by it, Senator Ralph Yarborough was instrumental in establishing the Special Subcommittee on Bilingual Education as part of the Senate Committee on Labor and Public Welfare. He chaired this new committee and, along with Senators Jacob Javits of New York, Robert Kennedy of New York, Joseph Montoya of New Mexico, John Tower of Texas, Jennings Randolph of West Virginia, and Harrison Williams of New Jersey, co-sponsored the first bill for bilingual education in the history of the United States.[18]

Any teacher or teacher educator entering the bilingual/bicultural education field should be familiar with the two volumes of hearings before the Special Subcommittee. These hearings were held in Washington, D.C., California, Texas, and New York. Supporters and testimony for the proposed national bilingual legislation came from all walks of life: students, parents, teachers, professors, and administrators; local, county, state, and national officials; representatives of the U.S. Congress; representatives of the business community; and other professionals. In other words, support came from across the board—geographically, politically, and educationally—in support of bilingual/bicultural education.

The hearings on the proposed bilingual education legislation were significant for a number of reasons. Yarborough's opening words convey the message:

> We have been able to discover with staff research and other investigation, this is the first hearing Congress has ever conducted into the problems of bilingual education. I was surprised to learn of this. The problems associated with educating children whose first language—first in terms of the order in which the child learns the language—is a language other than English, are serious, important, and deserving of attention.[19]

(b) *U.S. Senate Subcommittee on Equal Educational Opportunity.* The Subcommittee on Equal Educational Opportunity hearings, conducted by Senator Walter Mondale of Minnesota, gave further support to the need for bilingual/bicultural education for the linguistically and culturally distinct child/student. Although the Subcommittee had been in existence for some time, its major concerns were with White and Black America. Even in its consideration of the impact, effects, and problems of the national Emergency School Aid Act (formulated to help with desegregation) it seldom, if ever, addressed itself to the broader educational opportunities of the linguistically and culturally distinct student who was not Black or White.

This Subcommittee extended its interest to include attention to the educational problems and needs of Mexican Americans, Puerto Ricans, and Native Americans, which was to have later significance in extension of the Emergency School Aid Act. This time clear provisions were made for the needs of linguistically and culturally distinct communities which had not been included in the original legislation. Even more significant than this is the fact that when the 1974 unanimous Supreme Court decision was made in *Lau v. Nichols*, the Emergency School Aid Act established the 10 centers referred to above to implement the educational program and in-service and preservice teacher, counselor, and administrator training to meet the stipulations of *Lau v. Nichols*.

(c) *Other U.S. Commission on Civil Rights Hearings and Reports.* The above-mentioned contributions of the Civil Rights Commission illustrate its concentration on the largest Spanish-speaking community in the United States, the Mexican Americans. The broader concern of the Commission for quality and equity in educational opportunity for the linguistically and culturally distinct child/student was demonstrated by a number of works and hearings relating to other linguistically and culturally distinct communities, such as Native Americans, Puerto Ricans, Asians, and Blacks. Certainly the expansiveness of the application of bilingual/bicultural education is found in *A Better Chance To Learn*, which addresses itself to "language minority children." Without a doubt the authors of that document were very much influenced by the decision of *Lau v. Nichols* where the major thrust was the educational needs of 1,200 Chinese-speaking plaintiff children in San Francisco.

The Commission has held a number of major hearings in the last seven years to examine the educational needs of various minority communities in the United States. Such hearings established data relating to the unique, unmet educational needs of the linguistically and culturally distinct child. Thus, what was found to be serious for the Mexican American in the Southwest, as identified earlier by the NEA, was found to be true for other linguistically and culturally distinct communities and their children. Hearings were held in the following places (also see Appendix D):

Los Angeles, California, for the Mexican American (1968)
San Antonio, Texas, for the Mexican American (1968)
Boston and Springfield, Massachusetts, for the Puerto Rican (1972)
New York, New York, for the Puerto Rican (1972)
Window Rock, Arizona, for the Native American (1973)
Pismo Beach, California, for the Mexican American (1973)
Illinois, "Bilingual Bicultural Education: A Right or Privilege?" (1974)
Philadelphia, Pennsylvania, for the Puerto Rican (1974)
Washington State, for the Native American (1974)
San Francisco, California, for the Asian American (1975)

The data from these hearings and subsequent reports made the picture clearer: the current, traditional educational practices for the Mexican American and other linguistically and culturally distinct communities were not serving the unique educational needs of students from those communities. One of the most significant contributions of the Civil Rights Commission was to focus blame and responsibility on the educational system and away from the student and family. The latter had historically been held responsible by anthropologists, sociologists, and professional educators.

MAJOR EDUCATION LAWSUITS

The force which may have brought about the greatest progress for bilingual/ bicultural education, and to which such national entities as the NEA and the Civil Rights Commission contributed, were the education lawsuits that challenged the disproportionate placement of Mexican American and other linguistically and culturally distinct children in EMR classes.

In considering the developmental history of bilingual/bicultural education, it is essential that the teacher, counselor, administrator, and teacher educator study these significant lawsuits. They focused on educational problems at the beginning stages (ages 5 and 6) of a child's experience with the formal educational institution—the school.

These lawsuits were the first legal challenges to early testing, standardized tests, the selection process, and the caliber of instruction in EMR classes. In essence, they found that standardized tests were used to measure the capacity to know and speak English rather than a child's general achievement.[20]

The first of these EMR lawsuits—*Arreola v. Board of Education*—was in Santa Ana, California,[21] and was argued in state court. Although its impact was not as great as the case that followed, the Santa Ana case broke new legal ground. It focused blame where up to this point it had not been placed, brought about significant state legislation and subsequent state education policy, and generated important awareness of this type of educational neglect and damage to small children. Most significantly, the Santa Ana case paved the way for *Diana v. State Board of Education.*[22]

Unlike the Santa Ana case, *Diana v. State Board of Education* was argued in federal court. For the purposes of this study, the case established the groundwork for lawsuits described in the next section. The judgment of the court was that Mexican American and Chinese-speaking children already in classes for the mentally retarded must be retested in their primary language (unless they had previously been tested in it) and must be reevaluated only as to their achievement on nonverbal tests or sections of tests.[23]

Although this case was concerned with EMR classes, it became clear that it was the teachers, counselors, and administrators who were referring linguistically and culturally distinct children to such classes because, to quote one administrator, "We just do not know what to do with them."[24] The basis for most of the judgments which placed these children in EMR classes was their inability to speak or to function well in English, which had nothing to do with their mental or psychological capacities. It was evident that in too many instances the language and culture of the schools could not or would not adapt to the language and culture of a distinct community of pupils.

Diana v. State Board of Education was the forerunner of other EMR legal challenges won in California in behalf of Mexican Americans and Blacks; in Arizona, for Mexican Americans and Native Americans; and in Massachusetts, for

Puerto Ricans and Blacks. These cases pointed out dramatically that the educational system did not know how to cope with, train, or educate children of color. In this author's study of the issue, the characteristics of children misplaced in EMR classes are that, generally, they are of a given color, come from poor families, and speak no English, or the English spoken is not the formal English of the school; and the majority are girls.

The EMR lawsuits made their own impact on educational reform. Specifically, they contributed to acceptance of the notion that there was a serious problem, that it started very early in the child's life, that it had to do mainly with language and culture, and that what the schools were doing was not working for the linguistically and culturally distinct child. If anything, what the schools were doing was educationally and psychologically damaging to the child, and a new educational strategy had to be developed. The EMR cases, especially *Diana v. State Board of Education*, led to the development of what is commonly referred to today as the May 25th Memorandum.

The May 25th Memorandum (1970), Office for Civil Rights. This memorandum is the official policy of the Office for Civil Rights regarding responsibility of the public schools to provide for the educational needs of linguistically and culturally distinct students, in compliance with the 1964 Civil Rights Act and the 1968 elaboration. It was a direct result of *Diana v. State Board of Education.* The present acting director of OCR, Martin Gerry, attested to the direct impact of the "timing and content of the memorandum."

The May 25th Memorandum was intended to expand educational concerns and issues elaborated in the EMR cases. And it is apparent that until 1974 the majority of school district reviews in which the policy was applied concentrated on one issue—the educable mentally retarded. The four points of the memorandum are as follows:

1. Where inability to speak and understand the English language excludes national origin-minority group children from effective participation in the educational program offered by a school district, the district must take affirmative steps to rectify the language deficiency in order to open its instructional program to these students.

2. School districts must not assign national origin-minority group students to classes for the mentally retarded on the basis of criteria which essentially measure or evaluate English language skills; nor may school districts deny national origin-minority group children access to college preparatory courses on a basis directly related to the failure of the school system to inculcate English language skills.

3. Any ability grouping or tracking system employed by the school system to deal with the special language skill needs of national origin-minority group children must be designed to meet such language skill needs as soon as possible and must not operate as an educational dead-end or permanent track.

4. School districts have the responsibility to adequately notify national origin-minority group parents of school activities which are called to the attention of other parents. Such notice in order to be adequate may have to be provided in a language other than English.[25]

These four points set forth the Executive Branch's interpretation and illustrate the application of the 1964 Civil Rights Act as it relates to the education of linguistically and culturally distinct students who are unable to read, write, or comprehend English. This interpretation was extremely important in the growth of bilingual/bicultural education, since, as will be seen, it was the basis for the U.S. Supreme Court's unanimous 1974 decision in *Lau v. Nichols.* [26, 27]

OCR enforced its authority in three ways in reviewing a number of school districts:

1.   The national and regional offices reviewed school districts that had an evident problem of a high proportion of ethnic and racial minorities in EMR classes. Thus, school districts in California, New Mexico, Texas, Arizona, Kansas, Illinois, and Wisconsin were reviewed. From these reviews it became clear that the EMR issue was not relegated to one community (the Mexican American, which had raised it in the first place) but was spread across various linguistically and culturally distinct peoples—in essence, people of color.

2.   The national office pushed several lawsuits with the Justice Department in Beeville and Del Rio, Texas. In both instances an educational plan requiring bilingual/bicultural educational strategies was insisted on. Central to these two in-volvements of OCR was the expansion of its efforts from disproportionate EMR placement to the broader issue of the right to and provision of quality education for the linguistically and culturally distinct child. The emerging acceptable strategy under these circumstances was bilingual/bicultural education.

3.   Following *Lau v. Nichols,* which is discussed in the next section, OCR began to more aggressively pursue the issue of school district responsibility for taking "affirmative steps to rectify the language deficiency in order to open its instructional program" to the linguistically and culturally distinct child.

On January 23, 1975, OCR asked the chief state school officers in 26 states to help ensure that some "333 school districts provide equal educational opportu-nities to Spanish-surnamed, American Indian, Asian American and other national-origin minority students."[28] A review of the names of the states and the number of communities in each clearly shows that the need for bilingual/bicultural educa-tion cuts across the length and breadth of the United States. The 26 states are as follows:

Alaska	3*	New Jersey	10
Arizona	22	New Mexico	21
California	157	North Carolina	2
Colorado	15	Ohio	3
Connecticut	4	Oklahoma	5
Florida	6	Oregon	1
Illinois	1	Pennsylvania	3
Kansas	3	South Dakota	2
Louisiana	1	Texas	59
Maryland	1	Utah	5
Michigan	1	Virginia	2
Nebraska	1	Washington	2
Nevada	2	Wyoming	1

*Represents the total number of schools. Only in a few instances were ele-mentary or secondary schools indicated. The number in some cases is for whole cities, in others for school districts. The reason for the differences was not clarified.

The significant numbers of states and school districts also show the need for national concern for in-service and preservice training for bilingual/bicultural teachers.

OTHER SIGNIFICANT EDUCATION LAWSUITS

A number of education lawsuits in addition to the EMR cases have contributed significantly to the renaissance of bilingual/bicultural education. Without these lawsuits we would probably not be as far along in the general growth and acceptance of bilingual/bicultural education as we are. A brief discussion of the cases follows.

Serna v. Portales. This lawsuit was filed much earlier than *Lau v. Nichols.* However, the appeal from the U.S. District Court for the District of New Mexico (May, term 1974) was decided after *Lau.* Basically, the court supported the right of Mexican American students to equal educational opportunities and their right to be provided bilingual/bicultural education. The court ordered the formulation of a bilingual/bicultural education plan which would accommodate the language, history, and culture of Mexican American students in Portales. Interestingly enough, the court's order contained many of the features of the Civil Rights Commission's Mexican American Education Study.

Keyes v. Denver City Schools. In this decision the Tenth U.S. Circuit Court ordered the Denver schools to desegregate "root and branch." The Hispanic educators had submitted a plan that raised the question beyond just the moving of bodies and sought quality education for the Hispanic child. Thus, a master plan designed by Jose Cardenas[29] was submitted to the court and the Denver school system. The plan is built on the Cardenas-Cardenas theory of incompatibilities (developed by Blandina Cardenas and Jose Cardenas), which is that the typical public school program is basically incompatible with the linguistic and cultural needs of the linguistically and culturally distinct child. It identifies the basic incompatibilities and enables the schools to respond philosophically and programatically in providing quality, equal educational opportunity to the linguistically and culturally distinct child. (The Cardenas plan is described in more detail in Part II.)

Lau v. Nichols. This case was filed in San Francisco on March 24, 1970, on behalf of 1,200 Chinese-speaking children who were not being provided education programs in their language. The lower courts decided in favor of the defendant schools. However, in the appeal to the U.S. Supreme Court (in 1974) the latter decided unanimously in favor of the plaintiff children. The Court's statement will long have impact on the efforts to expand bilingual/bicultural education:

> Under these state-imposed standards there is no equality of treatment merely by providing students with the same facilities, textbooks, teachers, and curriculum; for students who do not understand English are effectively foreclosed from any meaningful education.

> Basic English skills are at the very core of what these public schools teach. Imposition of a requirement that, before a child can effectively participate in the educational program, he must already have acquired those basic skills is to make a mockery of public education. We know that those who do not understand English are certain to find their classroom experiences wholly incomprehensible and in no way meaningful.[30]

Whereas the debate for national bilingual education legislation occasioned the first public discussion on the topic in U.S. history, as was pointed out earlier, *Lau* was the first language case argued in the history of the Supreme Court.

There is much debate as to what *Lau v. Nichols* did or did not do for bilingual/bicultural education. It is the purpose here to place this historic decision in its rightful position of contributing significantly to the renaissance of bilingual/bicultural education. What is clear now is that *Lau* did not prescribe a specific remedy but ordered the San Francisco School Board to "refashion an appropriate relief." Justice Douglas touched on two possible choices:

1. The teaching of English to the students of Chinese ancestry who do not speak the language.
2. Giving instruction to this group in Chinese, while at the same time acknowledging that there may still be other choices.[31]

The petitioners in *Lau v. Nichols* built their case on a constitutional right to bilingual education. The Supreme Court avoided this issue by stating, "We do not reach the equal protection clause argument which has been advanced but rely solely on . . . the Civil Rights Act of 1964 . . . ."[32] The Supreme Court based its decision on the right, authority, and responsibility of OCR to determine policy outlining the affirmative responsibility of school systems to provide for the educational needs of the linguistically and culturally distinct student.

Aspira of New York v. Board of Education. On August 29, 1974, Judge Marvin E. Frankel signed a consent decree which directed that bilingual education in elementary, junior high, and high schools be provided by the New York City Board of Education. The principal beneficiaries of this would be Hispanic and, more specifically, Puerto Rican students.

Although the consent decree was a compromise between the Puerto Rican Legal Defense and Educational Fund and the New York City School Chancellor's Office, it ordered some significant actions, as follows:

All children whose English language deficiency prevents them from effectively participating in the learning process and who can more effectively participate in Spanish shall receive:

1. Intensive instruction in English
2. Instruction in subject areas in Spanish
3. The reinforcement of the pupils' use of Spanish and reading comprehension in Spanish where a need is indicated.[33]

In summary, therefore, court action has contributed immensely to the development of bilingual/bicultural education. The legal process is very slow and costly; in several instances it has taken from four to five years. But bilingual/bicultural education would not be where it is today without these lawsuits, for each contributed to the other in its own way. It is apparent that the courts are making more significant gains in providing quality education for the linguistically and culturally distinct student in the United States than are educators. An important danger is that the courts and the legislators will outdistance the educators and teacher educators in the race to provide quality, equal educational opportunity for the linguistically and culturally distinct child through bilingual/bicultural education.

Thus far we have examined significant causes for the renaissance of bilingual/bicultural education. Because great strides have been made in a relatively short time, it might be concluded that the bilingual/bicultural education movement has gone smoothly. Certainly this is not so. There has been and will continue to be great opposition to the concept, philosophy, and practice of bilingual/bicultural education. Both sides of the issue are discussed in Part II.

REFERENCES

[1] Fantini, M. D. *Public Schools of Choice: A Plan for the Reform of American Education.* New York: Simon and Schuster, 1973.

[2] Silberman, C. E. *Crisis in the Classroom: The Remaking of American Education.* New York: Vintage Books, 1970. p. 10.

[3] National Education Association. *A Relook at Tucson '66 and Beyond.* Report of a National Bilingual Bicultural Institute. Washington, D.C.: the Association, 1973.

[4] U.S. News and World Report. "Report from Capitol Hill: '75 Voting Act—Help for Those Who Don't Read English." *U.S. News and World Report* 52: 28; August 11, 1975.

[5] Casso, H. J. "A Descriptive Study of Three Legal Challenges for Placing Mexican American and Other Linguistically and Culturally Distinct Children into Educable Mentally Retarded Classes." Doctoral dissertation. Amherst: University of Massachusetts, 1972. (Unpublished)

[6] Arciniega, T. A.; de la Garza, R. O.; and Kruszewski, Z. A. *Chicanos and Native Americans: The Territorial Minorities.* Englewood Cliffs, N.J.: Prentice-Hall, 1973.

[7] Gerry, M. H. "Three Types of Discrimination in Minority Education." *Proceedings of a National Institute on Access to Higher Education for the Mexican American* (compiled and edited by Henry J. Casso and Marcia M. Bullard), Albuquerque, July 23-25, 1975. p. 34.

[8] National Education Association, Department of Rural Education. *The Invisible Minority.* Report of NEA-Tucson Survey on the Teaching of Spanish to the Spanish-Speaking. Washington, D.C.: the Association, 1966. p. v.

[9] *Ibid.*

[10] *Ibid.*

[11] *Ibid.*, pp. 17-18.

[12] Sanchez, G. "An Analysis of the Bilingual Education Act 1967-68." Doctoral dissertation. Amherst: University of Massachusetts, 1973. (Unpublished)

[13] U.S. Commission on Civil Rights. *Toward Quality Education for Mexican Americans.* Report VI: Mexican American Education Study. Washington, D.C.: the Commission, February 1974. pp. 67-68.

[14] *Ibid.*, p. 77.

[15] *Ibid.*, p. 79.

[16]U.S. Commission on Civil Rights. *A Better Chance To Learn: Bilingual Bicultural Education.* Washington, D.C.: the Commission, May 1975. p. 137.

[17]*Ibid.,* p. 139.

[18]Hearings Before the Special Subcommittee on Bilingual Education, Committee on Labor and Public Welfare. S428 Bilingual Education, Part I and Part II, January 17, 1967. U.S. Senate, Ninetieth Congress, First Session.

[19]*Ibid.,* p. 1.

[20]Casso, *op. cit.,* pp. 264 ff.

[21]*Arreola v. Board of Education,* Santa Ana Unified School District, 150577, California.

[22]*Diana v. State Board of Education,* Soledad, C70-37-RFP, California.

[23]Casso, *op. cit.*

[24]Casso, *op. cit.*

[25]Casso, *op. cit.,* Appendix H., p. 335.

[26]Alcala, C. "Legal Significance of *Lau.*" Paper presented at the National Education Task Force de la Raza and the Mexican American Legal Defense Fund *Lau v. Nichols* Conference, San Francisco, 1974.

[27]Gerry, *op. cit.*

[28]U.S. Department of Health, Education, and Welfare, Office for Civil Rights. News Release, January 23, 1975.

[29]Cardenas, J. A. "An Education Plan for the Denver Public Schools." Paper presented at the National Education Task Force de la Raza Conference, San Antonio, January 21, 1974.

[30]Gerry, *op. cit.,* pp. 1 ff.

[31]Alcala, *op. cit.,* p. 4.

[32]Alcala, *op. cit.*

[33]*Aspira of New York, Inc. v. Board of Education of the City of New York,* 58 FRD 62 (1973).

II. THE CONTROVERSY IN BILINGUAL/BICULTURAL EDUCATION: MELTING POT VS. CULTURAL PLURALISM

Shored up by its educational institutions, U.S. society in general has clung to and furthered the melting pot concept, which envisioned that the multivarious linguistically and culturally distinct peoples who were here or who came from other countries would mold or be molded into the "oneness of the all-American person." Although we may look different in ways we cannot do anything about, we as a people should all be alike. We should eat alike, behave alike, and learn alike.

Most administrators, counselors, teachers, and teacher educators have been trained under the melting pot theory, which is now being challenged. The changing of many deep attitudes and long-standing practices will be necessary, and in the process, rough spots will, naturally, be encountered.

From the data presented in reviews, hearings, studies, and lawsuits it is becoming clear that it was the people of color, especially those with the combined factor of language different from English, who did not "melt." Because of the efforts to more accurately understand the differences as well as the similarities among individuals, we are acquiring more knowledge about the learning styles of different peoples,[1] a factor hitherto not dealt with.

SOURCES OF RESISTANCE TO BILINGUAL/BICULTURAL EDUCATION

Nonacceptance of the Failure of the Public Schools

There is a strong unwillingness by some to accept the fact that the public schools have failed in the formal education of so many linguistically and culturally distinct children. New data are pointing up that failure. From this author's own studies, it is estimated that 225,000 psychologically sound children have been misplaced in EMR classes because of language and culture. Add to that the problems of early-grade retention, overageness, reading slowness, and the drop-out rate. Historically, the schools have blamed the students and their parents. Today the schools are also being blamed. At the heart of the question is the preparation of teachers, counselors, and administrators, as well as history and the curriculum.

Certainly the evidence of failure to educate many youngsters has necessitated an alternative educational strategy. It is in this vein that bilingual/bicultural education is offered, not as *the* alternative or as a panacea, but as one alternative strategy.

Fear of and Opposition to Change

Change in any institution, even in life itself, is difficult to accept, and this is particularly true in public education. As far as the growth and acceptance of bilingual/bicultural education is concerned, it is beset by an added feature—a 200-year history of a monolingual, monocultural, and ethnocentric thrust in the public schools. There were even periods when such phrases as "Be American, Speak English" had their impact on those who could not speak English. We have all been acquainted with school personnel who strongly voice the position, "We have done this for 200 years, why change now?" or "I learned it, so can you," or "I had to give up my language and culture, so can you." We are aware of many ethnic groups in this country the vestiges of which remain only in museums.[2]

A lesson from current data is that, if so many "made it, notwithstanding," what contributions could so many more have made if their learning styles had been recognized, if their language and culture had been used in the development of learning rather than regarded as a stumbling block. From the data mentioned earlier, whatever we have done in the public schools for the past 200 years for the education of the linguistically and culturally distinct child has not been as bene-ficial as it could have been. Bilingual/bicultural education is offered as a change, a new hope and alternative based on respect for language, culture, and homelife of the linguistically and culturally distinct child.

Fear of Job Displacement by Regular Teachers

For the first time in the history of the United States there is a surplus of teachers, currently estimated at 200,000. This oversupply comes at a time when there is a heavy demand for competent bilingual/bicultural teachers, counselors, and administrators at all levels.

In the area of language, the federal government has spent considerable money on training teachers of English as a Second Language (ESL). In many areas of the country, ESL teachers feel they should become the bilingual teachers in those school districts and states pushing forward with bilingual/bicultural education. What is needed, however, are teachers, counselors, and administrators who not only can communicate in a given second language but who understand the philosophical, pedagogical, and methodological process of bilingual/bicultural education. The ESL portion is exactly that, a portion of a more comprehensive educational strategy complementing and not set apart from bilingual/bicultural education.

In too many instances, the growth of bilingual/bicultural education has had to face the hard economic and social realities of supply and demand. A number of school districts (e.g., Milwaukee, Wisconsin, and St. Paul, Minnesota) have taken bold steps, notwithstanding the two realities mentioned above.

A Strong Negative Feeling Toward "Anything Foreign"

This feeling may be lessening because of our growing dependency on coun-tries we have not had to depend on historically, such as those in the Middle East and South America. However, although this nation is made up of immigrants, original "foreigners," there is a strong negative attitude toward anything which even smacks of being foreign. This is especially true with regard to language use in the public schools. Remember the chant, "Be American, Speak English." What was really meant by this?

The 1974 report of the Civil Rights Commission declared that throughout the Southwest "the language and culture of Chicano children are ignored and even suppressed by the schools."[3] Bilingual/bicultural education has had to and con-tinues to overcome this type of major obstacle to growth. One of the significant residual benefits of U.S.-Chinese détente was *Lau v. Nichols,* which benefited bilingual/bicultural education immensely. One speculates what would have been the decision had *Serna v. Portales* gone to the Supreme Court.

Although the above-stated situation is changing today, the fact is that many educational policies, practices, and attitudes emanate from the negative position described.

CRITICS AND SUPPORTERS OF BILINGUAL/BICULTURAL EDUCATION

Teacher Groups

Lawrence Wright, in "The Bilingual Education Movement at the Cross-roads,"[4] singles out a former president of the New York City local of the American Federation of Teachers, and vice-president of the New York State United Teachers, as one of the most vocal reactors against trends in bilingual education. According to Wright, some of the reasons for the AFT spokesman's opposition stem from the following:

1. He calls "bicultural" a "code word" for the hiring of more Spanish-speaking teachers
2. He opposes the compulsory features of some legislation mandating bilingual programs.
3. He contends that some bilingual programs are not truly bilingual.
4. He doubts many parents "want bilingual education for their children"
5. He questions the hypothesis that bilingual education "presumes to ease a child's entry into school."[5]

As was pointed out earlier, the NEA has been a significant contributor to and supporter of bilingual/bicultural education. It has supported the national legislation and appropriations, laying much of the groundwork through such able leadership as Monroe Sweetland.[6] The NEA also filed an amicus curiae brief in the *Lau v. Nichols* Supreme Court suit. The brief stated:

> The practical exclusion of any large group of children from public education, because of factors for which the children themselves are not responsible, is a matter of the gravest concern to those who . . . are interested in the education of American children.[7]

The Media

The *New York Times* of March 12, 1975, in an "Issue and Debate" article on bilingual education in that city, presented the positions of supporters and critics alike. This article recognized the compulsion of the consent decree formulated in the federal courts as a result of *Aspira v. Board of Education* and said that bilingual education will be a reality for the country's largest school district. The article's description of the significance of this fact supports a major premise of this author, i.e., that dramatic changes have occurred in (a) the historical, traditional practice of educating the linguistically and culturally distinct child, and (b) the role the schools and education have had in the assimilation of immigrants. To quote from the article:

> The adoption of bilingual education in New York City . . . the one that has borne a large responsibility for laying the foundations of assimilation for generations of immigrant Americans, is seen by both supporters and detractors as a major shift in public education here.[8]

The *Times* article illustrates the following position that this writer presented to some four hundred teachers and support staff participating in the March 1974 Bilingual Leadership Training Institute in Los Angeles:

> With the San Francisco *Lau v. Nichols* and the New York *Aspira* . . . law suits, the philosophy of Bilingual Bicultural Education will be applied in significant ways. It is my opinion that the battle for Bilingual Bicultural Education (although begun in other places and other communities) will be fought in these two places—San Francisco, California and New York, N.Y.[9]

The *Times* article presented the position of bilingual/bicultural education supporters from an educational-progress, positive-self-image, positive-desire-to-learn-English perspective:

> Bilingual education is viewed by its advocates as a way of allowing students to progress in subject areas—mathematics, science, social studies—without having to wait until they gain proficiency in English . . . the approach can help young people preserve their cultural identity and awareness, as well as proficiency in their ancestral language.
>
> The ability to function in English is a goal of bilingual education. Children who are products of good bilingual programs can be as capable of participating in the dominant English-speaking society as those youngsters who come out of regular monolingual curriculums [with] the advantage of a second language . . . .[10]

The teacher and teacher educator must realize that there obviously exists a clear-cut controversy in bilingual/bicultural education. The controversy is healthy, since it will bring out the best thinking to clarify where we have come from and where we are going in public education's response to the educational needs of the linguistically and culturally distinct child. In this controversy, the *New York Times* points out, the "main fear [of critics of bilingual education] is the possibility that, once a student is assigned to a bilingual program, it may become a permanent feature of his education, rather than. . .being phased out once he is proficient in English."[11]

Should this position be carried out to its logical conclusion, it would be possible for a student to participate in a bilingual program even into college or university. The opponents feel that such a plan would undermine the melting pot concept of the public schools. The proponents, however, ask the pointed question, "Why not?"

As was pointed out previously, a spokesman for the New York City arm of the American Federation of Teachers opposed bilingual education. This group is said by the *Times* to approve of "imparting skills to non-English-speaking students in their native language, but. . .it does not want the program to lead to 'ethnic separatism.' " It fears that there will be "hiring of bilingual teachers on the basis of ethnic quotas, political patronage, or other nonmerit considerations."[12]

A widely circulated and often-quoted column by Stephen Rosenfeld, entitled "Bilingualism and the Melting Pot," appeared originally in the *Washington Post* on September 27, 1974. Rosenfeld began his column with the following statement:

> With practically no one paying heed, the Congress has radically altered the traditional way by which immigrants become Americanized. No longer will the public schools be expected to serve largely as a "melting pot," assimilating foreigners to a common culture. Rather, under a substantial new program for "bilingual" education, the schools—in addition to teaching English—are to teach the "home" language and culture to children who speak English poorly.[13]

Rosenfeld went on to say that bilingual/bicultural education "rode into law on a tide of widespread and uncontested awareness that children who arrived in school speaking English poorly tended to do poorly in school." He further felt that bilingual/bicultural education was objectionable for two reasons:

> First, it is not clear how educating children in the languages and culture of their ancestral homeland will equip them for the rigors of contemporary life in the United States . . . . [Second] Bilingualism springs from a very different idea of America than what the public institutions of this country have accepted in the past.[14]

The work of Nathan Glazer, *Ethnicity and the Schools,* is quoted by Rosenfeld in raising the question, is "the current wave of ethnic feeling which seems now to be sweeping over America—the wave which carried bilingualism into public policy—weakening the common American glue and aggravating ethnic tensions and differences?" Glazer, Rosenfeld said, is of the position that "the assimilationist ideology of the melting pot is under strain, and he is frankly alarmed."[15]

Rosenfeld's column was picked up by other newspapers across the country. Then, Washington columnist Andrew Tully followed Rosenfeld's release with an article under the title "Education Is Raped." The Tully position also appeared in many papers, including the *Albuquerque Journal*. Tulley based his article on that of Rosenfeld.

Important for our consideration is the impact of the *Washington Post* on education policymakers, not only in the Executive and Legislative Branches of the federal government, but throughout the country. As to the *Albuquerque Journal,* it is the leading newspaper in New Mexico, which has a majority-minority population with the largest combination of Mexican Americans and Native Americans, growing numbers of whom are supporting bilingual/bicultural education. Moreover, New Mexico's language and history antecedes that of the East Coast, where generally the melting pot assimilationist position originated. Bilingual/bicultural education is in conflict with the powerful media positions of Rosenfeld and Tully, who side with the melting pot assimilationist point of view.

Tully states in his article:

> Well, I do not know "ethnic self-respect," but in my day the aim of what were then called "foreigners"—and sometimes worse—was to earn the respect of the English-speaking majority, not to proudly proclaim their aparthood. They did this the hard way, by learning to converse in the tongue of their adopted land, and by seeing to it—frequently by resort to the switch—that their kids did the same.

30

Tully goes on to justify his position by writing:

> We're all immigrants, including the snooty descendants of the Mayflower riffraff and excluding the American Indian. But for better or worse, most of the early settlers spoke English and so it was adopted as America's official, native language. This is not a form of discrimination against immigrants who speak another language, it is a fact of American life.

Tully associates speaking English with Americanization and seems to question the basic American loyalty of those who promote bilingual/bicultural education, or the art of communicating and comprehending in two languages:

> While it is natural and admirable for an "ethnic" child to look back proudly at his national heritage, his first duty to himself is to become Americanized as fast as possible.

In showing his own feeling toward the bilingual education movement, Tully erroneously attributes to Senator Cranston a position most people familiar with bilingual education's developmental history will take grave exception to:

> Senator Alan Cranston, D.-Calif., who fathered the bilingualism-in-schools monstrosity, says he had to do it to eradicate "an anti-minority tradition in American public education." What a lunatic fatuity! All the law does is dress our system of free schooling for all in a clown's suit.[16]

On the same date as Rosenfeld's column, John E. Hinkle, Jr., vice-president and general manager of WISN Radio in Milwaukee, reacted to complaints there and in Chicago about school administrators "failing to respond to the needs of their students":

> As this station sees it, the ethnic heritage of our citizens is one of America's most priceless possessions. Unless we can trace our ancestry to the American Indian—all of our forefathers came from another country.
>
> We like to believe America is something more than a "melting pot." We're the only nation on earth to share the advantage of all cultural backgrounds.
>
> But our forefathers didn't come here to remake America in the image of their native land. Mostly, they came here to escape the oppresssion of an older world.
>
> Because our language happens to be English, new arrivals to our country found it necessary to learn it. If you and I decided to move our families to another country, we wouldn't expect the schools of France or Germany or Italy to hire English-speaking teachers to accommodate our children.[17]

It is the opinion of this writer that Hinkle was influenced by Rosenfeld.

Finally, on the occasion of the public release of the Civil Rights Commission's major document on bilingual/bicultural education—*A Better Chance To Learn: Bilingual Bicultural Education*—in May 1975, the *Albuquerque Tribune* opposed the concept of bilingual education and sided with the assimilationist melting pot school of thought:

> However lofty its motives, the U.S. Civil Rights Commission is giving impractical advice by urging bilingual education for the millions of children who enter U.S. schools without being able to speak English.

> As should be obvious, this approach to education could handicap a child—
> perhaps permanently—by offering him a crutch that won't hold up in the
> work-a-day world in which he must live in later life.[18]

As can be seen, the growth of the current bilingual/bicultural education movement, although dramatic, has had opposition from various quarters, from educators and noneducators alike. It has grown nevertheless, and has already left its impact on behaviors and attitudes of the past. The impact is reflected in current notions of quality, equal educational opportunity, diversity in education, and fundamental acceptance of a culturally pluralistic educational and societal frame. This period of growth for bilingual/bicultural education can be called by whatever term one wishes—crossroads (Wright), renaissance (Casso). However, American public education has changed in its teaching attitudes and process, and bilingual/bicultural education as an educational strategy, philosophy, and process will have to be dealt with.

It is clear, therefore, that there are strong forces for and against the current renaissance of bilingual/bicultural education. The fundamental difference is philosophical, dividing along the lines of (a) the melting pot assimilationist position, and (b) the cultural pluralist position. We cannot discount the division, however, which is caused by basic fear—fear of the new, fear of change, fear of the other, fear of the different, or just plain fear.

Educators

Rupert Trujillo, in his address to the National Bilingual Bicultural Institute, gave an example of educators' support for the melting pot assimilationist position by quoting Cubberly, a famous educator in the early 1900's:

> Everywhere these people settle in groups or settlements to set up their na-
> tional manners, customs and observances. Our task is to break up these
> groups or settlements, to assimilate and amalgamate these people as part of
> our American race and to implant in their children so far as can be done, the
> Anglo-Saxon conception of righteousness, law and order, and our popular
> government, and to awaken in them a reverence for our democratic institu-
> tions and for those things in our national life which we as a people hold to be
> of abiding worth.[19]

In studying this statement, one wonders which institution Dr. Cubberly was referring to "to assimilate and amalgamate these people." What processes was he referring to when he spoke of implanting in "their children . . . the Anglo-Saxon conception of righteousness, law and order, and our popular government"? If Dr. Cubberly was speaking of the then-accepted role and function of public educational institutions, it seems understandable why the current data on educational achievement of linguistically and culturally distinct children/students are such, and more, why there is serious question as to the success of the melting pot school of thought.

During the public hearing the Civil Rights Commission conducted in San Antonio, Texas, in 1968, a junior high school principal was asked why he thought the data for Mexican American students projected such a dismal picture and about his views as to the possible relationship with genetic factors. He responded:

I am not an historian, but I would say that in the feeble knowledge that I have of history and looking at it from the past 2,000 years, Western Europe has been a battleground, and certainly where armies trample you have genes remaining. And the very measuring stick that we are trying to use here today is fundamentally a product of Western Europe's culture transplanted in America, and that is the measuring stick that we are trying to measure the Mexican American by.[20]

Castaneda,[21] reviewing the works of Cole and Cole (1954), pinpoints the melting pot philosophy to an exclusivist Ango-conformity position founded in racial superiority, exclusionist immigration policies, and a desire to maintain English institutions, the English language, and English-oriented cultural patterns. Assimilation is viewed as desirable only if the Anglo-Saxon cultural pattern is taken as the ideal. Castaneda considers the melting pot cultural phenomenon as something distinctly American. Developing his observation of "superiority," he quotes the American educator and philosopher John Dewey (1916) as saying:

I wish our teaching of American history in the schools would take more account of the great waves of immigration by which our land for over three centuries has been continuously built up, and made every pupil conscious of the rich breadth of our national make-up. When every pupil recognizes all the factors which have gone into our being, he will continue to prize and reverence that coming from his own past, but will think of it as honored in being simply one factor in forming a whole, nobler, and finer than itself.[22]

There are increasing numbers of educators and public-policy persons who are promoting the cultural pluralism position in the educational process and in the training of teachers, counselors, and administrators. In this writer's opinion, the growth and acceptance of the cultural pluralist position today is a significant contribution of the Mexican American community in particular and the bilingual/bicultural education movement in general.

Mario Fantini, presently dean of education at the State University of New York at New Paltz, poses the problem in today's teaching and clearly states his position:

Public school systems, in order to be equitable to the public, have tried to render all public schools identical. By manipulating all learners toward the same model, the school, instead of equalizing educational opportunities, has produced the exact opposite for many students and teachers.[23]

On the other hand, Fantini states:

Our concept speaks to openness. It values diversity, it is democratic, it embraces human growth and development, and it is unswerving in its recognition of individual worth.[24]

Stent and Hazard, writing their observations on an Education Professions Development Act (EPDA) conference on cultural pluralism in education, had this to say:

The melting pot ideology has failed. Society is splintered and the youth of America desperately are seeking their identity. Cultural pluralism is both a fact and a concept which has not been given due recognition. The fact that the United States includes citizens of diverse cultures cannot be challenged. The extent to which the non-white cultures have been disenfranchised or made invisible varies but their existence is a fact. Treated as bare fact, cultural pluralism means very little. Moving from fact to concept, however, opens the door to useful examination. Once cultural pluralism is viewed conceptually as well as affectively, its implications for education and teacher education can be explained.[25]

Blandina Cardenas, director of the San Antonio, Texas, Law Center, is confident of the working of the cultural pluralism position. She states:

> I really believe that cultural pluralism will be a functional response to this country. I think that most feel that cultural pluralism will work only to the degree that we lessen the gaps between groups in terms of material and educational and cultural success and acceptance. The longer we have to operate with large gaps between cultural groups, the longer we will have to be dealing with the fears and the defense mechanisms of the haves and the have-nots. If Mexican Americans, Franco-Americans, Italo-Americans feel more secure in their own cultures, not only culturally but socially and materially as well, we could all begin to function as a culturally pluralistic society and accept each other and assist each other in promoting our biculturalism or multiculturalism.[26]

Underlying the growth of the bilingual/bicultural education movement is the thought and philosophy of cultural pluralism. As has been noted, at challenge is the melting pot school of thought, which has its roots in the early thinkers, policymakers, and educators of this country.

Although there were advocates of the cultural pluralism position even at the turn of the century, it was not until the early 1970's that the strong, frequent, broad-based, articulate, cacophonus voices became effective.

While, as Gordon pointed out in 1964, "a central issue in Cultural Pluralism concerns the right of a minority ethnic group to preserve its cultural heritage without at the same time interfacing with 'the carrying out of standard responsibilities to general American civil life' " (cited by Castaneda[27]), the unique feature that has emerged in the last few years is a right, not only to preserve one's cultural heritage, but to preserve it through public education. This process is carried out through bilingual/bicultural education, which is a function of the state. The right has emerged as a result of the admitted failure of the American public school system to educate the linguistically and culturally distinct child. This admission lays bare the challenge that the melting pot philosophy has failed. Both promotion of and resistance to bilingual/bicultural education in the classroom, the school building, or the university will generally fall into one of these two schools of thought.

THE CARDENAS-CARDENAS THEORY OF INCOMPATIBILITIES

Given that the inability of the public school to respond meaningfully to the educational and developmental needs of the linguistically and culturally distinct child/student has its roots in the philosophical base of the melting pot assimilationist position, it is well to examine an actual school system and the problem areas posed in application.

Earlier, in examining significant lawsuits, the *Keyes v. Denver* desegregation case was mentioned and reference was made to the Cardenas-Cardenas theory of incompatibilities and the plan presented by José Cardenas to the federal court. The latter studied what he called the "cumulative deficit" or "progressive decline" phenomenon as indicated by data presented by the Denver Public Schools. The schools were convinced that one of the important features of upward socio-economic mobility was participation in public education. Cardenas suggested that the longer a minority child/student remained in school, the farther he/she fell behind the White, Anglo, middle-class student. (This writer found the same condition in interviews with investigators of New York public schools, in a major review conducted by OCR/HEW. In this case, the students concerned were Puerto Ricans and Blacks.)

Cardenas was courageous enough to focus this apparent failure away from the "home situation, lack of discipline, absence of stimulation by parents, and verbal deficiencies to the very instructional programs of the schools." He developed his education plan on two important points:

1. There are distinct learning characteristics and styles of the linguistically and culturally distinct child/student.
2. Failure, measured by the school, is attributed to the incompatibility of instructional programs with these distinguishable, unique educational characteristics.[28]

Thus, if an instructional program of the public school is developed for a White, Anglo-Saxon, English-speaking, middle-class school population, it follows that the program is incompatible with the characteristics of the linguistically and culturally distinct child. For success of the student and the instructional programs, each must fit the other as much as possible.

Focusing on the assumption of incompatibility, Cardenas proceeded to identify five basic areas where an instructional program can be incompatible with the learning characteristics of the linguistically and culturally distinct child/student: poverty, culture, language, mobility, and societal perceptions.

1. *Poverty.* Should the instructional content and process be geared to the middle class, and should the characteristics of the minority and majority student populations living in poverty not be taken into consideration, then the instructional program is incompatible with the learning characteristics of those students. If the teacher presupposes that each child beginning first grade has the same middle-class background and begins the educational process with a White, Anglo, middle-class-oriented and referenced-based curriculum, then a child from the lower socioeconomic or poverty environment starts off from day one on an unequal footing.

2. *Culture.* In describing the dysfunctionality of most instructional programs of public schooling with the linguistically and culturally distinct child, Cardenas makes three generalizations:

1. Most school personnel know nothing about the cultural characteristics of the minority school population;

2. The few school personnel who are aware of these cultural characteristics seldom do anything about it, and

3. On those rare occasions when the school does attempt to do something concerning the culture of minority groups, it always does the wrong thing.[29]

Frank Angel,[30] president of New Mexico Highlands University, in his presentation to the National Institute on Access to Higher Education for the Mexican American, observed that such professions as anthropology and sociology are identifying the cultural characteristics of various minority communities, but there is seldom an effort to develop educational programs along the lines of the characteristics identified.

A major thrust of bilingual/bicultural education strategy is to recognize the cultural characteristics of the participating students, their home, and community and then to build the learning experiences around these features. Then, the cultural characteristics of the linguistically and culturally distinct child, parent, and community (diet, costume, ethics, social patterns, and language) are perceived as strengths instead of weaknesses.

3. *Language.* Language is one of the elements of culture, according to Aragon.[31] In the bilingual/bicultural education renaissance, the promoters have distinguished the two characteristics of language and culture in the title of the movement. There is considerable debate concerning the use of the two terms. The present effort of bilingual/bicultural education is concerned with learning and developing in two languages, with and through a high regard for the culture of a child/student, his/her parents, and the community. Many teachers are leery of the term *bicultural,* since it is taken by some to mean, "You have to be of the same ethnic or racial background as the language/ethnic group involved. For example, in the Mexican American bilingual/bicultural program, the teacher must be fluent in English and Spanish and be Mexican American." This point is such an issue that it may be one of the major reasons why some ethnic or racial communities who are monolingual in English are more prone to push for the term *multicultural education.* But *bicultural* and *multicultural* need not be philosophically and pedagogically mutually exclusive; rather, the two terms are indicative of the same goals.

Bilingual/bicultural education has developed since the late 1960's because of the realization that children cannot learn in a foreign language. The language and information of the school must be learned through the language and information of the child and his/her home. A fundamental question about the purpose of education is whether the essential function of the school is to impart knowledge and information or to teach the child the language of the school and country. Without doubt, the traditional practice of schools has been to teach the child English first, then content. The effects of such a process are a high rate of grade repetition, overageness, and underachievement (U.S. Commission on Civil Rights, Mexican American Education Study). Bilingual/bicultural education theory suggests that both learning a language and learning information can occur together and advantageously in the learning process.

The question arises about ESL programs in which the United States has invested many educational dollars. The ESL educational approach is a good example of a strict language program without the cultural components, offered as an educational solution for the linguistically and culturally distinct child/student. Challenges to the effectiveness of ESL programs are probably best described in the briefs of the plaintiff children/students in the *Aspira of New York v. Board of Education* lawsuit. A study of these briefs reveals that the plaintiff Puerto Rican children entered ESL programs knowing only Spanish and left them after two or three years illiterate in both English and Spanish. The same problem occurred in Boston, reported in *The Way We Go to School*[32]; and Andersson and Boyer refer to the problem in their two-volume work, *Bilingual Schooling in the United States.*[33]

The question is not whether either ESL or bilingual/bicultural education should be adopted and the other discarded but what the role of each method is. ESL is an important program which is only one component of a total comprehensive educational strategy. Comprehensiveness is a goal of bilingual/bicultural education; therefore, ESL should fit into the design of the comprehensive bilingual/bicultural program in the educational strategy for the linguistically and culturally distinct child.

Cardenas suggests that there are three basic elements of a bilingual program which speak to this point:

1. The continued cognitive development of the child, with accompanying development of basic skills and content acquisition in his dominant language;
2. The development of English as a second language, and
3. The further extension of [the student's] native language system.[34]

The two incompatibility areas of culture and language are cited in the conclusions of the Civil Rights Commission's Mexican American Education Study. The Commission states:

- Chicanos are instructed in a language other than the one with which they are most familiar.
- The curriculum consists of textbooks and courses which ignore the Mexican American background and heritage.
- Chicanos are usually taught by teachers whose own culture and background are different and whose training leaves them ignorant and insensitive to the educational needs of Chicano students.[35]

The same problem occurs in the education of some Native American teachers who have participated in several of this author's graduate courses in intercultural relations. A number have expressed their complete unpreparedness to function in educational settings that include the Native American student. The problem certainly needs further study; however, the point here is that what has been learned by teachers, counselors, and administrators preparing to work with Mexican American children and students applies equally well to the educational needs of other linguistically and culturally distinct children.

4. *Mobility.* Mobility of students and families is a significant feature of contemporary American life. If an instructional program does not consider mobility, then (as Cardenas points out) that would be another incompatibility factor. Cardenas offers a solution to the reality of a high-mobility factor: the development of a mobile curriculum or highly individualized instructional program.

5. *Societal Perceptions.* Much has been written regarding the focus of the instructional process on the middle-class Anglo-Saxon child. It is generally accepted that such an instructional process excludes linguistically and culturally distinct children and that, when the latter are included, the weaknesses of the child/community are portrayed rather than the strengths. Such children have not gained a positive, reassuring self-image through the educational process of the school. The U.S. Commission on Civil Rights gives an example of this:

> The curriculum which the schools offer seldom includes items of particular relevance to Chicano children and often damages the perception which Chicanos have gained of their culture and heritage.[36]

In the extreme case, if a teacher, school, or school system must make the choice of a child knowing English or having a positive self-image and speaking the native language of his/her home, then the latter choice should be supported. A person who feels good internally will respond to societal needs in a more aggressive and successful manner.

What has been the role of the teacher in the area of societal perceptions? This question poses the subject of the next section.

TEACHER-STUDENT INTERACTION

A basic premise of this writing is that the renaissance of bilingual/bicultural education is due in great part to new data concerning the educational relationship between the school and the linguistically and culturally distinct child. The Cardenas theory of incompatibilities pinpoints critical areas of that educational environment and process. In view of the fact, however, that this review is concerned particularly with bilingual/bicultural teacher preparation, it is important to look at some significant research in the area of teacher-student interaction. The most critical part of education is what takes place between the teacher and the class, the teacher and each student, and especially the teacher and the linguistically and culturally distinct child. On the national, regional, state, or local level, all the new legislation, appropriations, and programs are for naught unless there is a healthy, positive, effective interaction between the teacher and his/her class, the teacher and individual students.

Recent research by the Civil Rights Commission provides keen insights for the bilingual teacher educator and the teacher in bilingual/bicultural education. In March 1973, the Commission's Mexican American Education Study report, *Teachers and Students*, was released. The report was a result of a modification of the Flanders Interaction Analysis System (FIAS) to determine the kinds of interaction between teacher and class, and between teacher and each student, as they related to identifiable ethnic or racial variables.

Teachers and Students sought to determine whether and to what extent there was a difference in interaction between teacher and Anglo child and teacher and Mexican American child. The research is significant for two reasons: (a) It was the first time the FIAS was adapted to determine interaction on ethnic and racial variables. (b) It identified specific, critically important areas where teachers need to develop an appreciation of the characteristics of linguistically and culturally distinct children/students and the concomitant skills to be effective in the educational development of all children.

The research was done in three states: California, New Mexico, and Texas. It included 52 rural, urban, and suburban schools—10 in New Mexico, 22 in California, and 20 in Texas—and data suitable for analysis were obtained from 429 classrooms observed.[37] Twelve categories of behavior were examined for possible interaction disparities. They are identified as "statistically significant" or "not statistically significant."[38] Although 6 of the 12 were found to be not statistically significant, from a teacher-preparation and teacher-educator perspective, these behavior areas are now identified and need careful attention. The categories are:

> Statistically Significant
> > Praising or encouraging
> > Acceptance or use of student ideas
> > Questioning
> > Positive teacher response
> > All noncriticizing teacher talk
> > All student speaking
>
> Not Statistically Significant
> > Acceptance of students' feelings
> > Lecturing
> > Giving directions
> > Criticizing or justifying authority
> > Student talk—response
> > Student talk—initiation

Specifically, the research found that there were:

1. Disparities in *teacher praise or encouragement*.

   Teachers make sparing use of praise and encouragement generally. But the average Anglo received about 36 percent more praise or encouragement than the average Mexican American pupil in the same classroom.[39]

2. Disparities in *acceptance or use of student ideas*.

   The average Anglo pupil in the survey area hears the teacher repeat, or refer to, an idea he or she has expressed about 40 percent more than does the average Chicano pupil.[40]

3. Disparities in *teacher questioning*.

   The average Anglo pupil in the survey area receives about 21 percent more questioning from the teacher than the average Chicano pupil.[41]

4. Disparities in *positive teacher response*.

   . . . the average Anglo pupil receives about 40 percent more positive response from the teacher than does the average Chicano pupil.[42]

In this category, the report elaborated by saying that "because positive teacher response represented overall warmth and approval, this disparity is also indicative of differences in the emotional tone of teacher relationships with Anglo and Chicao pupils."

5. Disparities in *all noncriticizing teacher talk.*

Teachers spend 23 percent more time in all nondisapproving talk with Anglo than with Chicano pupils.[43]

6. Disparities in *all student speaking.*

The average Anglo student spends about 27 percent more time speaking in the classroom than the average Chicano student.[44]

Although the second group of teacher-student disparities from a research perspective are not statistically significant, for purposes of achieving greater understanding of the interaction between teacher and linguistically and culturally distinct children it is important that in these six areas some disparity does exist, that there is difference of treatment in the kind and caliber of interaction that affects the learning environment, and that the disparities "indicate patterns of interaction favoring Anglos over Chicanos."

7. Disparities in *acceptance of students' feelings.*

Teachers expressed very little acceptance of the feelings of any students, but they did express acceptance twice as often for Anglos as for Mexican Americans.

8. Disparities in *lecturing.*

The average Anglo pupil received 20 percent more of this "teacher talk" classified as lecturing than did the average Chicano pupil.

9. Disparities in *giving directions.*

Teachers also spent more time relating information to Anglo pupils than to Chicano pupils.

10. Disparities in *criticizing or justifying authority.*

Although the differences in direction and criticism are small they are important as part of the total pattern of classroom interaction—a pattern in which Chicano pupils consistently are encouraged less and discouraged more than their Anglo counterparts.

11. Disparities in *student talk—response.*

... the average Mexican American verbally participated less in the classroom, both in response to the teacher and on his own initiative than the average Anglo.

12. Disparities in *student talk—response.*

> The average Anglo pupil observed talked about 23 percent more in response to the teacher than the average Chicano pupil. He also spent approximately 30 percent more time talking on his own initiative, than the average Chicano pupil.[45]

The picture is clear when all 12 of the identifiable categories of disparity are taken as a whole. It is not difficult for educators to conclude that the Chicano child receives unequal educational treatment in the schools of the Southwest. In terms of quantity and quality, the present system of education provided by the schools is monolithic, monolingual, and monocultural. It is true that the research is based on one culturally and linguistically distinct community. But this author's research on disproportionate placement of linguistically and culturally distinct children in EMR classes[46] lends support to the hypothesis that such data can be applied wherever Chicano children can be found in significant numbers throughout the United States, and to other linguistically and culturally distinct communities.

REFERENCES

[1]Ramirez (1974), cited in Castaneda, A. "Persisting Ideologies of Assimilation in America: Implications for Psychology and Education." *ATISBOS: Journal of Chicano Research*, Summer 1975. pp. 79-91.

[2]Howe, H. "The Cowboy and the Indians." Paper presented at the Texas-Mexican American Conference on Educational Opportunities, Southwest Educational Laboratory, Austin, 1968.

[3]U.S. Commission on Civil Rights. *Toward Quality Education for Mexican Americans.* Report VI: Mexican American Education Study. Washington, D.C.: the Commission, February 1974. p. 1.

[4]Wright, L. "The Bilingual Education Movement at the Crossroads." *Phi Delta Kappan* 55: 183-86; November 1973.

[5]*Ibid.,* p. 186.

[6]Sanchez, G. "An Analysis of the Bilingual Education Act 1967-68." Doctoral dissertation. Amherst: University of Massachusetts, 1973. (Unpublished)

[7]Wright, *op. cit.,* p. 186.

[8]Maeroff, G. I. "Issue and Debate: Bilingual Education Plan for City's Schools." *New York Times,* March 12, 1975.

[9]Casso, H. J. "The Implications of *Lau v. Nichols.*" Paper presented at the Bilingual Leadership Training Institute, Los Angeles, March 2, 1974. p. 3.

[10]Maeroff, *op. cit.*

[11]Maeroff, *op. cit.*

[12]Maeroff, *op. cit.*

[13]Rosenfeld, S. "Bilingualism and the Melting Pot." *Washington, Post,* September 27, 1974. p. A18.

[14]*Ibid.*

[15]*Ibid.*

[16]Tully, A. "Education Is Raped." *Albuquerque Journal,* October 7, 1974.

[17]Hinkle, J. E. Jr. "Student Walkouts." (Editorial) WISN Radio, Milwaukee, September 27, 1974.

[18]Albuquerque Tribune. "Two-Language Teaching." (Editorial) *Albuquerque Tribune,* May 19, 1975. p. 54.

[19]Trujillo, R. "Bilingual Bicultural Education: A Necessary Strategy for American Public Education." *A Relook at Tucson '66 and Beyond.* Report of a National Bilingual Bicultural Institute. Washington, D.C.: National Education Association, 1973. p. 21.

[20]Hearings Before the U.S. Commission on Civil Rights, San Antonio, Texas, 1968. p. 149.

[21]Castaneda, A. "Persisting Ideologies of Assimilation in America: Implications for Psychology and Education." *ATISBOS: Journal of Chicano Research,* Summer 1975. p. 80.

[22]*Ibid.,* p. 82.

[23]Fantini, M. D. *Public Schools of Choice: A Plan for the Reform of American Education.* New York: Simon and Schuster, 1973. p. 35.

[24]*Ibid.,* p. 3.

[25]Stent, M. D., and Hazard, W. "Cultural Pluralism and Schooling: Some Preliminary Observations." *Cultural Pluralism in Education: A Mandate for Change.* (Edited by Stent, Hazard, and H. Rivlin.) New York: Appleton-Century-Crofts, 1973. p. 13.

[26] Cardenas, B. "It's a Circle for Everybody To Be Involved In." *Education in Church and Society* 5: 20; 1972.

[27] Castaneda, *op. cit.,* p. 82.

[28] Cardenas, J. A. "An Education Plan for the Denver Public Schools." Paper presented at the National Education Task Force de la Raza, San Antonio, January 21, 1974. p. 8.

[29] *Ibid.,* p. 11.

[30] Angel, F. "Beyond Access: Designing Programs for Mexican Americans in Higher Education." Paper presented at the National Education Task Force de la Raza, Albuquerque, 1975.

[31] Aragon, _____. "An Impediment to Cultural Pluralism." *Cultural Pluralism in Education: A Mandate for Change, op. cit.,* p. 79.

[32] Task Force on Children Out of School. *The Way We Go to School.* Boston: Beacon Press, 1971.

[33] Andersson, T., and Boyer, M. *Bilingual Schooling in the United States.* Vols. I and II. Austin: Southwest Educational Development Laboratory, January 1970.

[34] Cardenas, J. A., *op. cit.,* p. 15.

[35] U.S. Commission on Civil Rights, *op. cit.,* p. 68.

[36] U.S. Commission on Civil Rights, *op. cit.,* p. 67.

[37] U.S. Commission on Civil Rights. *Teachers and Students: Differences in Teacher Interaction with Mexican American and Anglo Students.* Report V: Mexican American Education Study. Washington, D.C.: the Commission, March 1973. pp. 46-47.

[38] *Ibid.,* pp. 17-18.

[39] *Ibid.,* p. 21.

[40] *Ibid.,* p. 29.

[41] *Ibid.,* p. 37.

[42] *Ibid.,* p. 33.

[43] *Ibid.,* p. 39.

[44] *Ibid.,* p. 40.

[45] *Ibid.,* p. 18.

[46] Casso, H. J. "A Descriptive Study of Three Legal Challenges for Placing Mexican American and Other Linguistically and Culturally Distinct Children Into Educable Mentally Retarded Classes." Doctoral dissertation. Amherst: University of Massachusetts, 1972. (Unpublished)

III. IMPLICATIONS FOR BILINGUAL/BICULTURAL TEACHER TRAINING

To the administrator who said, "We just do not know what to do with them" (linguistically and culturally distinct children), to teacher educators, and to concerned teachers, the promoters of bilingual/bicultural education say, we have an alternative. The Cubberly philosophy has not been effective for the linguistically and culturally distinct child. We must learn from the past and develop new strategies with philosophies such as that of Fantini.[1]

The contemporary renaissance of the bilingual/bicultural education movement, then, is a response to principles the educator has voiced for some time: take a child as he/she is; build on strengths, not weaknesses; go from the known to the unknown; and respect the human person and his/her traditions and style of thinking, learning, and becoming.

GUIDELINES FOR IMPROVEMENT OF TEACHER TRAINING

There have been some efforts made to assure better preparation for teachers and administrators of bilingual/bicultural programs. Four such efforts are noted here.

What Teachers Should Know About Bilingual Education

Zintz, with assistance from project directors Ulibarri and Cooper, wrote *What Teachers Should Know About Bilingual Education* in 1969, setting forth objectives, principles, and cautions. These nationally and internationally renowned educators have vast experience in teaching Mexican Americans, Hispanos, Native Americans, and students of Latin American countries. For them, and very apropos today, six principles should guide the bilingual teacher:

1. Instruction in the first years of school should begin in the mother tongue . . . .
2. Bilingualism need not adversely affect school achievement . . . .
3. The emotional feelings about one's language are very important . . . .
4. To preserve a language, it needs to be used as a medium of instruction in the schools . . . .
5. While the members of a minor language group must learn the major language in order to function in the basic institutions of that society (government, economy, education, welfare), the reverse of this is not true . . . .
6. Native languages of minority groups are apt to be lost if: they serve no purpose in economics and commerce; radio and TV programs are not presented in that language; they are not used in the schools; there is no printed literature of importance in that language; and if progress in school places no reward on knowing that language.[2]

It is the hope of these educators and others who support this philosophy that the systematic and effective use of these six principles will bring about at least 12 major accomplishments:

1. The learner will become more proficient in his own oral and written language as well as in the second language.
2. The learner's achievement [in content areas] and aspiration levels will be raised through the program.
3. The learner will be recognized as one who represents "a culture within a culture."
4. The learner will be more capable of accepting democratic principles as a social process.
5. The school environment will become more adept at encouraging the bilingual to demonstrate the values of both the new and the old cultures.
6. The school will provide programs for children of different cultures.
7. The learner will become more proficient in oral language development in both languages.
8. A plan for optimum individual development will be provided through various types of teaching techniques.
9. The school environment will provide an atmosphere of understanding which encourages the learner to develop all facets of his personality.
10. The guidance program will aid the bilingual in seeking and preparing for success in both cultures.
11. The learner's self-concept will be consistently considered by the school.
12. The society which the learner accepts as a second culture will recognize the value of bilingualism. [3]

In the area of second-language acquisition, these educators stressed the importance of the teacher in a bilingual/bicultural program having a working knowledge of and personal commitment to seven linguistic principles, as follows:

1. Language is oral . . . .
2. Language is habit. It is learned behavior . . . .
3. Language is arbitrary . . . .
4. Language is personal.

(This principle particularly reflects student self-image. Critical, then, is the first approach of a teacher, who will contribute greatly to the positiveness or negativeness of that image. In too many instances data show that the enthusiasm of many teachers to teach English obliges linguistically and culturally distinct children to choose between the positive images of the family or the school. Children should not have to make that choice.)

5. The language of a given group of people is neither "good" nor "bad"; it is communication.

(There have been so many written complaints in this area that teacher preparation institutions, especially language departments, should examine the conflict. The common complaint, for example, in Spanish is, "Well, yes, you speak Spanish, but not the way it is spoken in Mexico or in Puerto Rico." Worse yet, "Yes, you speak Spanish, but not 'Castilian.' ")

6. Language is more than words . . . .
7. Language is culturally transmitted . . . .[4]

The Aspen Institute

In recognizing the rapid growth of bilingual/bicultural education programs, accelerated by *Lau v. Nichols*, and recognizing the slow response of teacher training institutions, a number of educators were convened in Aspen, Colorado, to assess the state of the art in undergraduate teacher training programs in bilingual/bicultural education. This institute was cosponsored by the Bilingual Leadership Training Institute at California State University, under the direction of Chuck Leyba, and the National Education Task Force de la Raza, under the direction of this author. The objective was to pull together professional expertise from various levels of involvement in teacher training for bilingual/bicultural education throughout the United States. Educators from the Native American, Puerto Rican, and Mexican American communities were represented. Our task was to develop responses to the following questions:

What should the teacher need to be able to do for maximum effectiveness in a bilingual/bicultural education program?

a. What knowledge would be required of the teacher to be effective in a bilingual/bicultural education program?

b. What skills would the teacher be required to have for effectiveness in a bilingual/bicultural education program?

c. What training experience would be recommended to help bring about this behavior, knowledge, and skills development?

The responses to these questions took the form of recommendations and were divided into (a) the cognitive domain and (b) the affective domain. The following list represents the consensus of the institute participants but is not intended to represent the total needs of a bilingual/bicultural training program.

A. Cognitive Domain

1. The teacher should have a working familiarity with the methodologies of teaching first and second languages.

   a. *Knowledge required.* This would require complete fluency in the two languages of the specific target population. Fluency in this case means an effective working knowledge of the grammatical structure, vocabulary, and literature of both languages, as well as the knowledge of process development in first and second language acquisition in becoming bilingual. The teacher must have a foundation in applied linguistics, sociolinguistics, and language development.

   b. *Skill required.* This would necessitate that the trainee be able to read, write, and speak both languages fluently.

   c. *Training recommended.* The training for the above should be divided into two parts: (1) academic and (2) field experience.
      (1) Academically, the teacher should be provided courses in first- and second language acquisition techniques and learning ap-

proach, as well as a course in process development in becoming bilingual.

(2) The field experiences should be directed experiences in a bilingual setting, including team teaching. Preferably the field experience ought to take place in the community in which the trainee is expected to teach. Possibly a part of the student teaching practicum could be in the form of a community internship.

2. The bilingual teacher should be able to diagnose language competency in the bilingual child.

   a. *Knowledge required.* To effectively diagnose language competency, the teacher should possess knowledge in diagnosis, interpretation, and application.

   b. *Skill required.* The skill to interpret and apply.

   c. *Training recommended.* A formal course in testing and measurement and field experience in diagnosis and application, preferably related to the bilingual community in which the teacher desires to work.

3. The teacher should be able to use the dialects of both languages of the children in the respective bilingual setting with fluency, understanding, and comprehension.

   a. *Knowledge required.* Fluency, understanding, and comprehension here would mean the possession of a working knowledge of both languages and dialects of the given community in which the program exists, as well as the knowledge of when to use each effectively in given education settings.

   b. *Skill required.* The trainee should possess the ability to recognize and identify the dialectal differences used by the students. The trainee should possess the ability to develop concepts through the dialects used, the ability to know when to use languages and related dialects, the ability to carefully identify for the students dialectal differences in their speech and the language of the curriculum materials.

   c. *Training recommended.* Familiarity with and skill in using the respective dialects could be acquired through a community internship, field experience, training films, guest lectures, and contact with community representatives familiar with dialectal differences, meaning, and application.

4. The teacher in the bilingual/bicultural education program must express favorable attitudes toward other languages and dialects and provide activities to develop these attitudes.

   a. *Knowledge required.* This would require knowing what constitutes favorable attitudes toward and familiarity with those activities which (though acceptable in the cultural environment of the teacher) may be construed as unfavorable by the culturally distinct community in which the bilingual teacher works.

b. *Skill required.* The trainee should be able to select those activities which demonstrate favorable attitudes toward the language, culture, family, and traditions of the students in his/her class. He/she should be able to communicate favorable attitudes, even in unfavorable situations.

c. *Training recommended.* This skill of demonstrating favorable attitudes even in unfavorable situations can be developed through field training, particularly in the community where the teacher will work. Lab situations can be made available. The student teaching program can provide the opportunity to apply the activities selected.

5. The teacher must use language styles which will further the bilingualism of the student. Status should be given to the language of the child and the school.

a. *Knowledge required.* The teacher should possess a keen knowledge and understanding of the goals and objectives of bilingual/bicultural education. The teacher in the bilingual/bicultural program should have a working knowledge of the relationships between language and culture, especially the language and culture of the school, home, and community of the child/student.

b. *Skill required.* The teacher should be able to provide educational activities which will make the child/student comfortable in learning the language and culture of the school, while at the same time building respect for the language and culture of the home/community of the child.

c. *Training recommended.* To acquire the knowledge and skill for this objective, lab-field training, especially in the community environment in which the teacher desires to work, is recommended.

6. The teacher in a bilingual/bicultural program should provide the learning environment and curriculum to enable the child to use two or more languages in the learning process.

a. *Knowledge required.* The teacher in a bilingual/bicultural program should have a knowledge of environmental references and related models applicable to the linguistically ahd culturally distinct child/ community and the class setting. The teacher should be aware of the emotional environment in his/her class, school, and community. He/she should know what constitutes a healthy, favorable climate for learning, given these variables.

b. *Skill required.* The teacher in this setting should have the implementation competencies to distinguish what is favorable for maximum learning in his/her given class/school, and be able to develop related curriculum models and educational activities to best utilize the favorable learning environment to the advantage of the bilingual child.

c. *Training recommended.* Formal classes to develop these skills can be provided by educational psychology courses dealing with appropriate curriculum models relative to a given target population, and courses in learning environments. Field experience can be provided by curriculum and training experiences, such as team teaching, individualized instruction, the integrated day concept, and use of culture in the curriculum.

7. The teacher in the bilingual/bicultural program should be able to use cross-cultural references in advancing the cognitive development of students. He/she should be able to use community resources in understanding the development of cultural resource material.

   a. *Knowledge required.* This will require that the teacher in the bilingual/bicultural program have a good knowledge of culture, of the material produced for the community he/she is teaching. This teacher should know what criteria to use in judging appropriate materials and what is needed in a resource center for the class and program. He/she should know about small-group learning. Further, he/she should know how to identify student levels in relation to materials available. He/she should know the relationship of teaching materials to cultural and curriculum goals. He/she should know the importance of community resources in developing cross-cultural curriculum and support material.

   b. *Skill required.* The teacher should be able to select appropriate curriculum and support materials for student development. He/she should be able to develop, adopt, and effectively use culturally related materials; be able to identify levels of materials in relation to the level of the student; and be able to evaluate the effective use of community in the development of cross-cultural curricula.

   c. *Training recommended.* Coursework in the nature and use of culture is important. Developing criteria and survey evaluation of material should be provided the teacher trainee, who should take courses in materials development and evaluation.

8. The teacher in the bilingual/bicultural program must be able to select cross-cultural references in advancing cognitive development.

   a. *Knowledge required.* The teacher must be knowledgeable in growth and development concepts and related themes for the monolingual and bilingual/bicultural child. The teacher must be well aware of existing and needed material in this field.

   b. *Skill required.* The trainee should be able to establish growth goals and be able to write a curriculum in relation to these goals.

   c. *Training required.* The teacher in a bilingual/bicultural program needs courses or modules in child growth and development, along with courses in classroom management.

9. The teacher in the bilingual/bicultural program should exhibit such sensitivity to the culture of the target group as to be able to judge between appropriate and inappropriate methodologies.

a. *Knowledge required.* The teacher should possess a working knowledge of the methodologies and cultural attributes of the target community.

b. *Skill required.* This working knowledge should provide the teacher with the skill to select and apply the appropriate methodologies for the identified cultural attributes of his/her class.

c. *Training recommended.* This knowledge and skill can be developed through field observation, especially of successful programs.

10. The teacher in the bilingual/bicultural education program should use tests appropriate to program objectives.

a. *Knowledge required.* He/she should have a working knowledge of testing instruments and their strengths and weaknesses, as well as knowledge of present evolvements and assessments.

b. *Skill required.* To accomplish this, the teacher should be able to identify tests applicable to the specific learning needs of the target population. The teacher should be able to diagnose the educational problems of a child, interpret tests, and prescribe a remedy.

c. *Training recommended.* Courses should be available for training in diagnostic techniques as well as training in application of the evaluation procedures.

B. Affective Domain

11. The teacher should develop self-confidence in the child/student of the bilingual class.

a. *Knowledge required.* The teacher in the bilingual program should be familiar with psychological principles regarding positive child learning and growth, have a positive self-image, have a positive image of children, know something about group dynamics, and know how to diagnose a child's abilities.

b. *Skill required.* The teacher in the bilingual program should be able to diagnose a child's abilities and provide successful learning experiences.

c. *Training recommended.* Workshops in self-esteem should be provided to the teacher trainee, as well as a course and experiences in group dynamics and values clarification. These experiences could be provided in small-group lab experiences.

12. The teacher in the bilingual/bicultural education program should have positive attitudes toward advancing the life pursuits of the students/ children and a commitment to raising their levels of aspiration.

a. *Knowledge required.* The knowledge required to apply this would be psychological (the maturational and aspirational characteristics and techniques of the target group served). The teacher should be familiar with child counseling and guidance techniques, both group and individual. He/she should be familiar with cultural factors in these techniques as they relate to learning. Finally, he/she should be aware of appropriate community role models.

b. *Skill required.* The teacher should be able to apply psychological techniques in the maturational pursuits, both individually and collectively, to apply counseling and guidance techniques, and to provide activities incorporating community role models.

c. *Training recommended.* Labs should be provided to allow the trainee the opportunity to observe and apply psychological techniques of motivating individual students and a class. The trainee should have practice in how to survey, identify, and utilize role models from the community served.

13. The teacher should structure programs that will foster positive attitudes in relating to others.

a. *Knowledge required.* Implementation will require the trainee to be familiar with psychological and sociological cultural foundations, i.e., have a knowledge of cross-cultural values, awareness of conflicting cultural mores, and knowledge of materials—audio, visual, or printed—in which these are demonstrated.

b. *Skill required.* The trainee should be able to identify cross-cultural collaborating or conflicting values, and to articulate these to students. The trainee should be able to discuss openly with students the conflicting values encountered in curriculum, media, and society.

c. *Training recommended.* The trainee should be provided the opportunity in lab work to identify and deal with conflicting cross-cultural values. Workshops can be provided in how to select and provide curricula and media.

14. The teacher should be able to effectively use in the child/student's learning process, the values, aesthetics, and view of nature that the child and his/her community respect and should relate the learning environment to the learning process.

a. *Knowledge required.* This would require that the trainee have a working familiarity with the local environment and know how to integrate this environment with learning.

b. *Skill required.* This requires the trainee to recognize the community environment characteristics and incorporate that recognition into the student/child's physical and intellectual development.

c. *Training recommended.* The trainee should be provided field experience in successful programs, followed by lab experiences for applying what he/she has learned.

15. The teacher should respect the child, be sensitive toward the child's sociocultural differences, and be alert to his/her effect on the child.

This outline is but a minimum of what is recommended for the teacher who wishes to be effective in a bilingual/bicultural education program.

Center for Applied Linguistics

The Center for Applied Linguistics (CAL)[5] has also compiled a set of qualifications for the bilingual/bicultural education teacher in eight major areas:

1. Language proficiency
2. Linguistics
3. Culture
4. Instructional methods
5. Curriculum utilization and adaptation
6. Assessment
   a. General
   b. Language
   c. Content
   d. Self
7. School-community relations
8. Supervised teaching.

The full description of these qualifications can be found in Appendix E.

Personal/Professional Checklist

For the teacher or teacher training institution that would like a simple checklist of personal characteristics and professional qualifications, the one that follows is by Dolores Gonzales from a work she and Casso prepared for an institute on the bilingual teacher and the open classroom.[6]

Criteria for the Selection of Teachers
for Bilingual/Bicultural Programs

	YES	NO
I. *Personal Characteristics*		
An effective teacher for a bilingual program demonstrates:		
1. The belief that cultural diversity is a worthy national goal.	___	___
2. A respect for the child and the culture he/she brings to school.	___	___
3. The conviction that the culture a child brings to school is worth preserving and enriching.	___	___
4. An awareness that cultural and linguistic differences are obvious *individual differences.*	___	___
5. A commitment to enhance the child's positive self-image.	___	___
6. A positive self-concept of his/her ability to contribute to a bilingual program.	___	___

I. *Personal Characteristics (continued)*	<u>YES</u>	<u>NO</u>
7. A willingness to learn more about bilingual education.	——	——
8. Flexible human relations.	——	——
9. A capacity to share ideas.	——	——
10. A confidence in children and their ability to learn.	——	——

II. *Professional Qualifications*

An effective teacher for a bilingual program demonstrates:

1. Competency and experience as an elementary school teacher.	——	——
2. A knowledge of areas related to bilingual education: English/Spanish as a second language, linguistics, etc.	——	——
3. Literacy in the Spanish language.	——	——
4. A facility in applying modern approaches to improve teaching of concepts and skills.	——	——
5. An ability and a resourcefulness in adapting materials to make them relevant to the child.	——	——
6. A readiness to participate in team teaching or other innovative organizational patterns.	——	——
7. An awareness of the implications of culture to learning.	——	——
8. A knowledge of research to explain what bilingual education is and why it is needed.	——	——
9. A willingness to work cooperatively with other adults (teachers, aides, parents, etc.) in a classroom setting.	——	——
10. A loyalty and a commitment to the objectives of an experimental program.	——	——
11. An interest in seeking new approaches to contribute to the experimental nature of the program.	——	——

It will be noticed that there is a similarity in the four sources used in this section (Zintz, Aspen, CAL, and Gonzales). In reviewing each of them, to avoid being left with the impression that the bilingual/bicultural education program is strictly for promotion of language or culture, it should be kept in mind that the language and culture of the linguistically and culturally distinct child are used to aid the school in its objective, the cognitive growth and development of the child.

TEACHER VIEWS OF BILINGUAL/BICULTURAL EDUCATION

During 1973-74, many states were having their first statewide bilingual education conferences and institutes. This author has tried to determine the thinking of teachers and administrators of bilingual programs who attended some of those conferences. The objective was to get a clearer picture of the thinking of teachers in relation to that of teacher educators in bilingual education. Surveys were conducted at the first National Bilingual Bicultural Institute,[7] held in Albuquerque, New Mexico, November 28 - December 1, 1973, and at follow-up state conferences in Arizona[8] and Wisconsin.[9] The findings presented here give a cross-section of participants' opinions about bilingual education and teacher preparation.

Although the greater concentration of bilingual programs is in the elementary grades, especially K-3, 66.9 percent of the Arizona bilingual conference respondents strongly supported the bilingual program being continuous from kindergarten through the twelfth grade, and 10.3 percent strongly disagreed. In the Wisconsin study, 81.2 percent of the participants strongly agreed and only 8.1 percent strongly disagreed. Among the National Institute respondents, 89.5 percent were in favor of a continuous K-12 program and only 5.9 percent against.

The concern of the president of the New York local of the American Federation of Teachers was noted earlier regarding the hiring of only bicultural teachers. On the question of recruitment and hiring of Spanish-speaking teachers as a high priority in the district or project area, 55.9 percent of the National Institute respondents strongly agreed, 21.3 percent strongly disagreed, 17.7 percent were in the middle, and 5 percent gave no response. In Arizona, 47.5 percent strongly agreed it was a high priority, 16.2 percent felt strongly it was not a priority, while 13.7 percent were indifferent. In Wisconsin, 59.8 percent of the respondents strongly agreed and 21.5 percent strongly disagreed.

Findings in the area of teacher preparation and the qualities a bilingual teacher should have were as follows:

Regarding the *personal qualities of a bilingual teacher,* 81.3 percent of the National Institute participants indicated these should be a high priority in the preparation program while 4.5 percent indicated a low priority. In Arizona, 76.3 percent of the respondents felt development of personal qualities for bilingual education was a high priority, and 2.9 percent considered it a low priority. Wisconsin had 86.6 percent for high priority and 2.6 percent for low priority.

In the area of a *teacher's knowledge of children and appreciation of the community from which the students come,* 95 percent of the National Institute respondents saw this as a high priority of teacher training and only 1.4 percent indicated it was a low priority. In Arizona, 82 percent considered it a high priority and 3.6 percent a low priority. In Wisconsin, 91 percent rated this as a high priority and 3.6 percent as a low priority.

On the question of *development of teaching skills,* 85 percent of the National Institute respondents rated this as a high priority and 4.6 percent as a low priority. In Arizona, 73.4 percent of the participants felt this was a high priority and 2.1 percent a low priority, while 11.5 percent were indifferent and 12.9 percent chose not to respond. In Wisconsin, 79.5 percent of participants noted this as a high priority, 6.3 percent as a low priority, and 10.7 percent were indifferent.

Regarding *whether the teacher preparing teachers for bilingual programs should be bilingual,* 90.5 percent of the National Institute participants felt that this was a high priority, 2.3 percent rated it as a low priority, 5.9 percent were indifferent, and 1.4 percent chose not to respond. In Arizona, 68.4 percent felt this was a high priority, 5.1 percent a low priority, 14.4 percent were indifferent, and 12.2 percent chose not to respond. In Wisconsin, 83.9 percent agreed this was a priority, while 6.3 percent disagreed.

RESPONSE OF TEACHER TRAINING INSTITUTIONS IN TRAINING BILINGUAL PERSONNEL

The bilingual/bicultural education movement has developed so rapidly that teacher training institutions have not sufficiently developed the programs necessary to meet current demands for personnel. That the need is great is indicated by such educators as Charles Leyba,[10] director of Project MAESTRO, California State University, who in 1973, estimated a need for over 35,000 bilingual/bicultural teachers. The Civil Rights Commission makes further reference to the current national need for bilingual/bicultural teachers:

> Because of the scarcity of trained and certified bilingual bicultural teachers, many bilingual bicultural programs have assumed the responsibility for designing and implementing their own teacher training programs.[11]

It seems clear that school districts cannot wait for state teacher training institutions.

The 1968 national bilingual education legislation and amendments passed in 1970 provided for preservice and in-service bilingual teacher training.[12] However, few universities and colleges developed undergraduate or graduate programs under this legislation. The reasons for this lack of commitment are not clear. If there was a weakness in the law itself, this was rectified in the 1974 Bilingual Education Act, which makes a heavy commitment to training and fellowships.

The need for teacher training in bilingual/bicultural education has been picked up by a number of states. Some, such as California, Texas, and Illinois, are beginning to allocate substantial money for preparation.

The state of the art in the area of bilingual teacher training was covered in the U.S. Civil Rights Commission's 1974 report, *Toward Quality Education.* The Commission randomly sampled 25 Southwestern teacher training institutions. The sample demonstrates conclusively the necessity for expansion of teacher education programs to meet bilingual teacher training needs.[13]

The great need for bilingual in-service and preservice teacher training is clear. The response by teacher training institutions has been slow, although a decade has passed since the renaissance of bilingual/bicultural education began and even though educators had identified the qualities, characteristics, and needs as early as 1969. A few reasons for this slowness are:

1. The country finds itself for the first time in its history with a great surplus of regular teachers, those who have been prepared to teach only the monolingual/ monocultural child/student.

2. The country and individual states are spending the greatest amount of educational dollars in their history. (New Mexico, for example, spends 75 cents of every tax dollar on education; and the federal education expenditure is second only to defense.) This spending, coupled with the great economic recession, demand for economic and educational accountability, and the national surplus of 200,000 teachers, has caused state legislatures to be more cautious in allocating more tax dollars to the preparation of teachers in general, notwithstanding the need for bilingual/bicultural teachers in particular.

3. There is a lack of recorded data on the progress, successes, and advantages of bilingual education programs to convince state legislatures of the benefits of such programs, which would justify drastic changes and utilization of new state funds. For example, Arizona has in the past year reduced its allocation for bilingual education.

4. The issue of the melting pot versus cultural pluralism philosophy applies critically to the response of teacher training institutions. It is the author's opinion that most administrators and teachers holding positions of leadership were trained in the melting pot school of thought. Therefore, those in charge of teacher training institutions may not be philosophically and ideologically committed to bilingual/bicultural education programs.

5. Where deans of teacher training institutions are committed to bilingual/ bicultural education, significant numbers of department chairpersons (such as elementary, secondary, early childhood, reading, curriculum and instruction) do not have the same philosophical commitment to (or worse, their priorities do not include) teacher training for bilingual/bicultural education.

6. Teacher training in institutions of higher education has not been coordinated with the teacher training needs of client state or local school districts. This lack of coordination means that different priorities are served, which contributes to the surplus of one set of teachers while at the same time exacerbating the shortage of bilingual/bicultural teachers. Reading specialists, curriculum developers, materials developers, educational psychologists, science teachers, and early childhood specialists are badly needed.

7. Some college of education department chairpersons perceive teacher training in bilingual/bicultural education as only a language program and attempt to shift the burden for teacher training onto the language departments.

8. There seems to be an apparent unwillingness, reticence, incapacity, and fear among university departments to work collaboratively, interdisciplinarily, and interdepartmentally to develop a comprehensive bilingual education teacher training program in cooperation with the needs of local school districts.

REFERENCES

[1]Fantini, M. D. *Public Schools of Choice: A Plan for the Reform of American Education.* New York: Simon and Schuster, 1973.

[2]Zintz, M. V. *What Teachers Should Know About Bilingual Education: An Interpretive Study on Bilingual Education.* Albuquerque: College of Education, University of New Mexico, March 1969. pp. 40-41.

[3]*Ibid.,* pp. 39-40.

[4]*Ibid.,* pp. 11-12.

[5]Center for Applied Linguistics. "Guidelines for the Preparation and Certification of Teachers of Bilingual/Bicultural Education." Arlington, Va.: the Center, 1974.

[6]Casso, H. J., and Gonzales, D. "Bilingual Bicultural Education: A Challenge to the Open Classroom Unit." A Manual prepared for the Teacher Training Institute, Washington, Connecticut, School District, Media Corporation, June 1974.

[7]Garcia, J. O., and Peralta, A. *An Evaluation of the National Bilingual Bicultural Institute.* Albuquerque: National Education Task Force de la Raza, College of Education, University of New Mexico, 1973.

[8]Casso, H. J., and Garcia, J. *An Analysis of the Evaluation of the Arizona First Bilingual Institute.* Albuquerque: National Education Task Force de la Raza, College of Education, University of New Mexico, 1974.

[9]Casso, H. J., and Garcia, J. *An Analysis of the Evaluation of the Wisconsin First Bilingual Institute.* Albuquerque: National Education Task Force de la Raza, College of Education, University of New Mexico, 1974.

[10]Leyba, C. F., and Casso, H. J. *Bilingual Teacher Training Fact Sheet.* Los Angeles: Project MAESTRO, California State University, September 21, 1973.

[11]U.S. Commission on Civil Rights. *A Better Chance To Learn: Bilingual Bicultural Education.* Washington, D.C.: the Commission, May 1975. p. 93.

[12]Sanchez, G. "An Analysis of the Bilingual Education Act 1967-68." Doctoral dissertation. Amherst: University of Massachusetts, 1973. p. 229. (Unpublished)

[13]U.S. Commission on Civil Rights. *Toward Quality Education for Mexican Americans.* Report VI: Mexican American Education Study. Washington, D.C.: the Commission, February 1974. pp. 36-39.

IV. A REVIEW OF ERIC PUBLICATIONS

Although attention has already been given to the desirable characteristics, knowledge, skills, and training of bilingual/bicultural teachers, this section is a review of literature related to teacher training other than that cited previously. Almost 250 publications, articles, presentations, and papers in the Educational Resources Information Center (ERIC) collection or indexed by ERIC were searched in hopes of identifying in-service and preservice bilingual teacher training models. (See Appendix G.) It was found that considerable literature exists on the need for and problems and characteristics of specific in-service and preservice programs; however, actual descriptions of bilingual teacher training models are almost nonexistent.

PRESERVICE BILINGUAL TEACHER TRAINING

Traditionally, teacher training institutions have prepared students for teaching by providing them with general education and methods courses. Actual work with children did not occur until the fourth or final year of their studies. This has been found to be inadequate preparation for teachers.

The review of the literature in this area shows little innovation in preservice training programs for students preparing to work with linguistically and culturally distinct students in a bilingual/bicultural education program aside from linguistics courses and sometimes a bilingual methods course. Still largely unidentified are the recommended specific components or content of courses and the relationship between theory and field work. One innovation, primarily influenced by the two-year Teacher Corps programs, is the inclusion of more intensive and extensive field work and community involvement throughout the bilingual training program. There has also been an increased emphasis on competency-based teacher education and the use of modules to develop the competencies needed by bilingual teachers.

Jackson[1] states that teacher quality is a greater factor in the achievement of minority-group children than in the achievement of majority-group children. It is the shared responsibility of training institutions, schools, and the community to keep teacher education programs responsive to current educational needs.

Most programs merely stress the use of an interdisciplinary training approach for bilingual teacher training which includes education, history, anthropology, sociology, psychology, and ESL. (See, for example, Mazon and Arciniega,[2] Ferguson and Bice,[3] Troike,[4] Michel,[5] Richburg and Rice,[6] Bernal,[7] Hughes and Harrison,[8] Valencia,[9] and the Library of Congress.[10]) There is general agreement on this interdisciplinary, interdepartmental collaboration in the training of bilingual/bicultural teachers. However, the literature is very weak in the description of how this training is to be done. Few models have been described in the ERIC documents.

The selection of trainees for bilingual teacher training programs does not seem to be carefully planned. Only one of the articles in the ERIC search, by Adler,[11] points out that the candidate cannot just be a native speaker to teach English or Spanish components of the bilingual program; he/she must have other qualifications. Others do not go into the specifics of reorganization recommendations but simply suggest (a) that we must make the course work more relevant, or (b) that curriculum innovations must be made within the professional courses (Jones[12]).

Only three authors cite specifics about including the child's and the community's culture in the bilingual teacher education program. Most of the coursework that Jones describes with relation to culture has to do with laboratory school work with ethnic and cultural lifestyles in relation to teacher education. Sandstrom[13] says only that we should have programs which serve to heighten awareness of culture and sensitivity to cultural differences. Richburg and Rice stress the need to develop cultural sensitization.

Interaction skills with students and communication on a broad base with many groups in society are very important. Richburg and Rice, Jones, and the University of Southern California[14] stress that the teacher education staff should be made more aware of human relations factors in education so that they can stress the development of these skills in their classes. This has direct implication for the emphasis of the bilingual/bicultural education teacher training movement.

More importance is now being placed on the role of the community in teacher education, as well as on the importance of the trainee's learning to work in the community and with the community in the teaching setting. (See Bauch,[15] Student National Education Association,[16] Kreidler,[17] and Wilson.[18] Also Sandstrom, and the University of Southern California.) There is little information available, however, on effective, successful use of the community involvement concept. The greatest involvement seems to be in assisting in cultural development (e.g., telling stories of folklore and history, and participating in advisory councils). Assisting in the critically important actual writing of bilingual curriculum materials is the area of least participation.[19]

More emphasis is being placed on increasing the on-site education of teachers, particularly in training for bilingual/bicultural programs. Such recommendations have been stressed by Guerra,[20] Dodd,[21] Hawkins,[22] and Flores.[23] The impact of the Teacher Corps community-learning models should continue to contribute substantially to furthering this concept.

Considerable attention is given to various types of methods in bilingual teaching. Most stressed, however, is the development of the teacher's personal interaction with students early in their education. Also necessary are intensive support and supervision, as well as great care in the selection of teaching models (Sandstrom, Student National Education Association, and Ferguson and Bice; also see California State College[24]). The findings in the U.S. Commission on Civil Rights report on student-teacher interaction (*Teachers and Students,* Report V, Mexican American Education Study) indicate this is a very important area which needs further attention.

It is increasingly recommended that field experiences take place (a) earlier in undergraduate bilingual teacher training programs, and (b) more frequently and more intensely as integral parts of teacher education or as methods of implementing good teacher education programs. Certainly the Teacher Corps and the Career Opportunity Program (COP) have contributed greatly toward this trend since, in both programs, half of the teacher training is through field experience. During these increased field experiences meaningful involvement in the sociodynamics of the community is stressed. (See Student National Education Association, Richburg and Rice, Sandstrom, Wilson, Kreidler, Jackson, Ferguson and Bice, and the University of Southern California.) In the area of field experience, there has been considerable criticism that trainees or bilingual student teachers are not placed with carefully selected master bilingual programs or teachers. Too often the bilingual trainee is left alone without on-site supervision. There is no incentive (such as academic credit for the master teacher) and, finally, the link with the home-base bilingual teacher training institution is weak. The growing emphasis on field experience, and its importance in the personal development of the trainee, will necessitate improving these areas for successful bilingual teacher training programs.

Recently there has been a trend toward competency-based teacher education and the employment of modules in developing teacher competency (Sandstrom; also American Association of Colleges for Teacher Education,[25] and Lindberg and Swick[26]). One of the strongest movers of the concept seems to be the Center for Applied Linguistics.[27] The impact of competency-based education on bilingual/ bicultural teacher training should be closely observed. New Mexico, for example, has recently dropped its effort to develop a teacher certification plan based on competency, notwithstanding a 1971 commitment to implement one by September 1975.

IN-SERVICE BILINGUAL TEACHER TRAINING

Many of the teachers already involved in bilingual education lack necessary skills. Even if they have general bilingual teaching skills, they may not be prepared to implement a specific bilingual program because they lack familiarity with the appropriate approaches, goals, and methods as well as with the community they will serve. Most teachers in bilingual programs today have been trained only in languages and not in other content.

The majority of the literature in this area is in the form of evaluations of Title VII programs. The evaluators have made very general recommendations for more in-service training, but the specifics of such training are not given. More needs to be written on the identified areas of in-service training.

Various approaches to in-service training have been suggested. Training may vary from one-day sessions every six weeks (Adkins and Crowelle[28]) to two hours (Goodman[29]) or even a one-day-a-week session throughout the year. The content of programs is not adequately detailed. The sources generally identify the topics to be covered only as culture, bilingual methods, and materials. On the other hand, the description of the New York City Board of Education[30] in-service program includes bilingual methodology, history of bilingual education, philosophy encompassing the total child, language arts in both English and Spanish, and bilingual instruction in all curriculum areas. Also included are culture, language proficiency classes, and bilingual workshops.

Specific instructional techniques, approaches, materials, aids, and modes of school organization appropriate for multicultural student groups are reported by Dykes.[31]

Instructional techniques, curriculum planning, technical assistance, and classroom methodology are stressed by Theimer[32] and also by Goodman, who adds team-teaching techniques and the use of an eclectic method.

Cultural environment, family and social group characteristics, teacher attitudes and characteristics, shortcomings of schools and suggestions for surmounting these shortcomings are topics explored in in-service preparation as described by Rubeck.[33]

Another aspect of in-service training is planning at the level of involvement of the in-service participant (Theimer), such as preschool or junior high.

The goals of a number of writers in the area of in-service training include the academic education of participants (Theimer); sensitivity to cultural variance; bilingualism (Goodman); practical "how to"; relationship of trust between trainer and teacher; encouraging trainees to be experimenters and innovators, learners, and problem solvers; and how to develop a sense of professionalism.[34]

Dominquez[35] reports on programs based on a teacher needs assessment, areas of interest, and community needs. These needs were dealt with through lectures, individual learning packages, encounter groups, seminars, small-group discussions, and workshops. Adkins and Crowelle also base in-service preparation on noted deficiencies and their correction, as does Washington.[36] The master teacher's role consists of personal discussions, evaluations, and development of curriculum materials.

Rubeck used outside consultants to observe and suggest program changes. In-service suggestions could also come from parent and student groups, as well as from faculty committees.

Adkins and Crowelle discuss observation of a teacher's language and lessons via tape, which is critiqued and discussed by the teacher and trainer. They also cite opportunities for teachers in bilingual programs to observe each other and to observe and evaluate taped lessons and compare their evaluations with actual lesson plans. Teachers can also discuss particular problems encountered in implementing the bilingual program and arrive at more effective methods of implementation. The supervising teacher can demonstrate lessons. Practice and role playing are used as corrective devices if the trainees need special assistance. They experience the actual making of lesson plans, discuss their pace of implementation, and plan future lessons.

RECOMMENDATIONS BASED ON THE ERIC SEARCH

Preservice Education

1. More emphasis should be placed on developing preservice models.

2. More emphasis should be placed on the recognition of learning styles (as documented by Castaneda[37] and Ramirez[38]), the development of cognitive processes, judgment, classroom procedures, and the development of interaction sensitivities which enable the teacher to gauge the optimum teaching moment for positive instruction.

3. More stress should be placed on setting up a responsive teaching and learning environment.

4. There should be a follow-up of graduates of the bilingual preparation program at any teacher training institution.

5. The teacher training institution should be held accountable for the preparation of teachers for bilingual programs.

6. Efforts should be made to recruit competent trainees and to assist them in completion of preservice programs.

7. Involvement of bilingual teacher trainees in actual school situations should begin early in their training.

8. Bilingual teacher trainees must receive the kind of training that will enable them to work effectively in bilingual/bicultural programs.

9. Language must not be the only requirement for training to work in bilingual/bicultural settings. Emphasis must also be placed on the affective and cognitive needs of the child within his/her culture and community.

10. Teacher training insitutions must develop comprehensive, ongoing, and first-rate bilingual preparation programs, from undergraduate through doctoral levels.

11. Preservice teachers in the bilingual education program must be trained to work with paraprofessionals.

12. There must be a standardized method of selecting cooperating master bilingual teachers.

13. Bilingual teacher trainees must be competent and willing to work in the community.

14. Bilingual teacher trainees must be given opportunities to observe teachers who work effectively with children in bilingual programs.

15. Research should be conducted to identify the kinds of preservice training that will result in effective bilingual/bicultural teachers.

16. Bilingual teacher trainees should have laboratory school work before being permitted to work with students in regular schools.

17. Assessment criteria must be developed to determine whether a bilingual teacher trainee is competent to work with linguistically and culturally distinct students before he/she is permitted to complete the program.

In-Service Education

1. Teachers, administrators, teacher educators, and the community should all be involved in the planning and evaluation of a bilingual in-service program. All participants should feel that the training is appropriate to their level and needs. Programs should be individualized and, in some cases, competency-based, so that certain demonstrable knowledges, skills, and behaviors of the participants can be evaluated.

2. In-service training should be required of all teachers, administrators, and paraprofessionals involved in a bilingual program. There should be separate-level meetings as well as all-level sessions so that all groups may be supportive of each other. A sense of team effort is important for implementing change.

3. All of the aforementioned could be utilized as content and situation demand, with continual experimentation and reassessment.

4. Interaction and communication skills should be stressed.

5. A needs assessment should be the basis of the developed bilingual in-service program.

6. In-service preparation for bilingual education should be conducted for at least six weeks during the summer for teachers who have not taught in the program, with at least one half-day session per week throughout the school year. There should also be weekly half-day visits to each classroom by the teacher trainer.

7. All the areas covered in preservice training for bilingual education should be ongoing in in-service preparation as well, but concentrated and adapted to the specific needs of teachers and community.

8. More research should be conducted to identify the kinds of in-service training that would be most effective for bilingual programs.

9. There is a great need to integrate theory and practice in in-service programs to make them more effective and successful.

10. The main goal of in-service training in bilingual/bicultural education should be to make the program more viable and to provide ongoing preparation for the teacher to be able to work more effectively with children in the cognitive, language, cultural, and personal domains.

11. In-service training should include student evaluation techniques, both pre- and posttesting, and prescriptive techniques based on test results.

12. There should be an ongoing evaluation of the bilingual/bicultural teacher training program.

REFERENCES

[1]Jackson, V. D. "A Descriptive Study of Teacher Education Programs for Navajo Indian College Students," 1974.

[2]Mazon, M. R., and Arciniega, T. A. "Competency-Based Education and the Culturally Different: A Role of Hope, or More of the Same?" (Preliminary draft.) Washington, D.C.: American Association of Colleges for Teacher Education, 1974.

[3]Ferguson, E. T., and Bice, G. R., editors. "Annual National Vocational-Technical Teacher Education Seminar Proceedings, Teaching Disadvantaged Youth (Third, Miami Beach, October 20-23, 1969), Final Report." Leadership Series No. 24. Columbus: Center for Vocational and Technical Education, Ohio State University, 1969.

[4]Troike, R. C. "Statement on Linguistic Concerns in Bilingual Education." Paper presented to the National Advisory Committee on the Education of Bilingual Children, Washington, D.C., January 1974.

[5]Michel, J. "The Preparation of the Teacher for Bilingual Education." Speech presented at Edinboro State College, Pennsylvania, September 1972.

[6]Richburg, J. R., and Rice, M. J. "Accountability in Minority Teacher Training: The University of Georgia Indian Teacher Training Program." Paper presented at the College and Faculty Association Section of the annual meeting of the National Council for the Social Studies, Boston, November 21, 1972.

[7]Bernal, E. M. Jr., editor. "The San Antonio Conference. Bilingual-Bicultural Education—Where Do We Go from Here? (San Antonio, March 28-29, 1969)." San Antonio: St. Mary's University, March 1969.

[8]Hughes, B. E., and Harrison, H. W. "Evaluation Report of the Bilingual Education Program: Harlandale Independent School District, San Marcos Independent School District, Southwest Texas State University, 1970-1971." San Antonio: Harlandale Independent School District, 1971.

[9]Valencia, A. A. "The Effects of a College Teacher Training Project with Emphasis on Mexican American Cultural Characteristics. An Evaluation Report." Sacramento, Calif.: Sacramento State College, September 1970.

[10]Library of Congress. "Language and Area Studies Programs and the Participation of Spanish and Portuguese Speaking Minorities in American Society." Report of a meeting held at Miami, Florida, May 1-3, 1969.

[11]Adler, E. F. "Basic Concerns of Teaching English as a Second Language in New Jersey." Speech delivered at the meeting of the Foreign Language Teachers Association, New Jersey Education Association, November 7, 1968.

[12]Jones, D. W., editor. "Human Relations in Teacher Education." Muncie, Ind.: Ball State University, August 1970.

[13]Sandstrom, R. H., editor. "Clash of Cultures: A Report of the Institute on the American Indian Student in Higher Education, July 10-28, 1972." Canton, N.Y.: St. Lawrence University, 1972.

[14]University of Southern California. "Teacher Corps, Urban, Cycle II. Final Program Report." Los Angeles: the University, 1969.

[15]Bauch, J. P. "Community Participation in Teacher Education: Teacher Corps and the Model Programs." GEM Bulletin 70-4. Athens: College of Education, University of Georgia, 1970.

[16]Student National Education Association. "New Teachers: New Education." Student Impact Occasional Paper. Washington, D.C.: the Association, 1970.

[17]Kreidler, C. J., editor. "On Teaching English to Speakers of Other Languages, Series II." Papers read at the TESOL Conference, San Diego, March 12-13, 1965.

[18] Wilson, H. B. "Quality Education in a Multicultural Classroom." *Childhood Education* 50: 153-56; January 1974.

[19]Casso, H. J., and Bernal, E. R. *A Preliminary Study of 5th Year ESEA Title VII Bilingual Programs with High Concentration of Mexican American Students.* Albuquerque: College of Education, University of New Mexico, 1974.

[20]Guerra, E. L. "Training Teachers for Spanish-Speaking Children on the Mainland." Address delivered at the Conference on the Education of Puerto Rican Children on the Mainland, San Juan, October 18-21, 1970.

[21]Dodd, W. J. "Address to the Opening General Session: Fifth Annual TESOL Convention, New Orleans, March 4, 1971."

[22]Hawkins, J. E. "Indian Education in the Bureau of Indian Affairs." Washington, D.C.: Bureau of Indian Affairs, U.S. Department of the Interior, 1972.

[23]Flores, S. "The Training of Bilingual-Bicultural Personnel." *Bilingual Education.* Proceedings of the Aspira National Bilingual Education Think Tank, March 1973. pp. 49-65.

[24]California State College. "Operation Fair Chance: The Establishment of Two Centers To Improve the Preparation of Teachers of Culturally Disadvantaged Students, Emphasizing Occupational Understanding Leading to Technical-Vocational Competence. Final Report." Hayward: the College, September 1969.

[25] American Association of Colleges for Teacher Education. "Excellence in Teacher Education: 1969 Distinguished Achievement Awards of the American Association of Colleges for Teacher Education." Washington, D.C.: the Association, 1969.

[26]Lindberg, D. H., and Swick, K. J. "Developing Creative Materials for Teaching the Culturally Different Child." Paper presented at the Annual Meeting of the Association of Teacher Educators, Chicago, February 23, 1973.

[27]Center for Applied Linguistics. "Guidelines for the Preparation and Certification of Teachers of Bilingual/Bicultural Education." Arlingtion, Va.: the Center, November 1974.

[28]Adkins, D. C., and Crowelle, D. C. "Field Test of the University of Hawaii Preschool Language Curriculum. Final Report." Honolulu: Educational Research and Development Center, University of Hawaii, 1970.

[29]Goodman, F. M. "Compton Bilingual Plan Review Report 1971-72." Compton, Calif.: Compton Unified School District, 1972.

[30]New York City Board of Education, Office of Bilingual Education. "Building Bridges to Better Bilingual Education." Brooklyn: the Board, 1973.

[31]Dykes, A. R. "Training Institute for Staff Members of School Systems with Multi-Cultural Schools." Memphis, Tenn.: Center for Advanced Graduate Study in Education, Memphis State University, 1966.

[32]Theimer, W. C. Jr., editor. "Career Opportunity Programs: Improving Opportunities for Success in Education." Stockton: California Laboratory of Educational Research, University of the Pacific, April 1971.

[33]Rubeck, R. F., and others. "A Guide for Urban-Teacher Development. Final Report." Columbus, Ohio: Battelle Memorial Institute, November 1970.

[34]Miller, J. O. "An Educational Imperative and Its Fallout Implications." Paper presented to President's Committee on Mental Retardation Conference, Warrenton, Va., August 10-12, 1969.

[35]Dominguez, F. "Bilingual Education: A Needs Assessment Case Study." Teacher Corps Associates, Resources for CBTE, No. 5. Santa Cruz: University of California, 1973.

[36]Washington, B. B. "Cardozo Project in Urban Teaching: A Pilot Project in Curriculum Development Utilizing Returned Peace Corps Volunteers in an Urban High School. Interim Report." Washington, D.C.: District of Columbia Public Schools, January 1964.

[37]Castaneda, A. "Persisting Ideologies of Assimilation in America: Implications for Psychology and Education." *ATISBOS: Journal of Chicano Research*, Summer 1975. pp. 79-91.

[38]Ramirez, M. "Potential Contributions by the Behavioral Sciences to Effective Preparation Programs for Teachers of Mexican-American Children." Paper prepared for the Conference on Teacher Education for Mexican Americans, New Mexico State University, February 13-15, 1969.

APPENDIX A

APPROVED BILINGUAL EDUCATION FELLOWSHIP PROGRAMS
(1975-1976)

Target Language	Degree Program	Number of Fellowships Available	Institution
Spanish	Ph.D.	14	Arizona State University, Tempe
		6	Boston University
		15	University of Houston
		10	University of Illinois, Urbana
		6	Kansas State University, Manhattan
		10	University of Massachusetts, Amherst
		25	University of New Mexico, Albuquerque
		10	New Mexico State University, Las Cruces
		10	Pennsylvania State University
		15	State University of New York, Albany
		10	University of Texas, Austin
		30	Texas A & I, Kingsville
		4	University of Washington
	Ed.D.	20	University of the Pacific, Stockton
	M.A.	18	Biscayne College, Florida
		3	California State University, Bakersfield
		21	California State University, Los Angeles
		15	Chicago State University
		20	Hofstra University, New York
		5	University of Kansas, Lawrence
		5	Michigan State University
		15	New Mexico Highlands University, Las Vegas
		15	Pan American University, Edinburg, Texas
		40	San Diego State University
		10	University of Texas, Austin
		5	University of Texas, El Paso
		8	University of Washington
		10	Wichita State University, Kansas
Greek	Ph.D.	5	Florida State University, Tallahassee
Spanish & French		30	New York University, New York City
Japanese & Chinese		20	Seton Hall University, New Jersey
Spanish & Cantonese	M.A.	50	California State University, Sacramento
Spanish & Italian		15	Fordham University, New York City
Native American		5	University of New Mexico, Albuquerque

Source: Office of Bilingual Education. The information has been rearranged specifically for this document.

APPENDIX B

OFFICE OF BILINGUAL EDUCATION GRANT AWARDS,
FEBRUARY 1975

STATE	LOCAL EDUCATION AGENCY (LEA)	CITY	AMOUNT
ALASKA	Alaska State-Operated School Systems	Anchorage	$ 500,000
	BIA Bethel Agency, Dept. of Interior	Bethel	204,850
ARIZONA	Papago Indian Agency	Sells	83,120
	Havasupai Tribal Council	Supai	29,000
	Tempe School District No. 3	Tempe	66,000
	Tucson Public Schools	Tucson	144,192
	IHE's		
	Northern Arizona University	Flagstaff	65,000
	Pima Community College	Tucson	70,000
	University of Arizona	Tucson	499,499
	University of Arizona	Tucson	70,000
	Chinle Public School District No. 24	Chinle	209,600
	Chinle Agency, BIA Cottonwood Day School	Chinle	50,000
	Rock Point School, Incorporated	Chinle	201,400
	Douglas Public Schools District No. 27	Douglas	120,000
	Flagstaff Public Schools	Flagstaff	68,549
	Apache County District Ganado Public School No. 19	Ganado	115,000
	Kayenta Public School District No. 27	Kayenta	133,490
	Nogales Public School District No. 1	Nogales	169,000
	Peach Springs School District No. 8	Peach Springs	44,220
	Phoenix Elementary School District No. 1	Phoenix	156,500
	Phoenix Union High School System	Phoenix	175,000
	Sacaton Public School District No. 18	Sacaton	95,500
CALIFORNIA	Arvin Union School District	Arvin	95,000
	Placer County Office of Education	Auburn	396,900
	Baldwin Park Unified School District	Baldwin Park	167,000
	Berkeley Unified School District	Berkeley	816,000
	Bonsall Union School District	Bonsall	62,617
	Calexico Unified School District	Calexico	190,300
	Capistrano Unified School District	Capistrano	102,000
	San Dieguito Union High School District	Cardiff	81,528
	Carpinteria Unified School District	Carpinteria	75,900
	ABC Unified School District	Cerritos	321,000
	Chino U.S.D.	Chino	109,135
	Sweetwater Union H.S.D.	Chula Vista	185,000
	Corcoran U.S.D.	Corcoran	56,500
	Corona-Norco Unified School District	Corona	146,000
	Jefferson Elementary School District	Daly City	103,020
	Delano Union Elementary School District	Delano	46,800
	Dos Palos Joint Union Elementary School District	Dos Palos	55,000
	Dos Palos Union High School District	Dos Palos	101,719
	Ravenswood City School District	East Palo Alto	100,200
	El Monte School District	El Monte	126,000
	Mountain View School District	El Monte	121,000
	Encinitas Union School District	Encinitas	27,000
	Etiwanda School District	Etiwanda	66,165
	Fremont Unified School District	Fremont	257,500
	Gilroy Unified School District	Gilroy	228,700
	Glendale Unified School District	Glendale	207,575
	Guadalupe Union School District	Guadalupe	68,948
	Gabrillo Unified School District	Half Moon Bay	28,381

Office of Bilingual Education Grant Awards, February 1975 (Continued)

STATE	LOCAL EDUCATION AGENCY (LEA)	CITY	AMOUNT
California (Continued)	Hayward Unified School District	Hayward	$ 220,137
	Hollister School District	Hollister	186,445
	San Benito Joint Union High School District	Hollister	181,229
	Oceanview School District	Huntington Beach	234,844
	Irvine Unified School District	Irvine	102,000
	La Habra City School District	La Habra	81,000
	Hacienda La Puente Unified School District	La Puente	242,737
	Lawndale School District	Lawndale	100,000
	Lennox School District	Lennox	156,450
	Los Angeles Unified School District	Los Angeles	1,458,500
	Morgan Hill Unified School District	Morgan Hill	43,000
	Newport-Mesa Unified School District	Newport Beach	68,000
	Newark Unified School District	Newark	93,535
	Norwalk-La Mirada Unified School District	Norwalk	166,000
	Oakley Union School District	Oakley	92,500
	Oceanside Unified School District	Oceanside	115,000
	Chaffey Union High School District	Ontario	110,000
	Ontario-Montclair School District	Ontario	200,000
	Orange Unified School District	Orange	144,000
	Oxnard School District	Oxnard	160,500
	Oxnard Union High School District	Oxnard	80,000
	Palm Springs Unified School District	Palm Springs	103,000
	Paramount Unified School District	Paramount	284,630
	Pasadena Unified School District	Pasadena	262,000
	El Rancho Unified School District	Pico Rivera	261,000
	Lucia Mar Unified School District	Pismo Beach	135,500
	Pittsburg Unified School District	Pittsburg	284,500
	Pomona Unified School District	Pomona	342,500
	Redlands Unified School District	Redlands	90,000
	San Mateo County	Redwood City	160,280
	Riverside Unified School District	Riverside	168,000
	Garvey School District	Rosemead	285,813
	Rowland Unified School District	Rowland Heights	194,000
	Sacramento City Unified School District	Sacramento	176,500
	Sacramento City Unified School District	Sacramento	207,000
	Salinas City School District	Salinas	214,650
	Salinas Union High School District	Salinas	233,832
	San Bernardino County Superintendent of Schools Office	San Bernardino	287,200
	San Diego Unified School District	San Diego	292,694
	San Francisco Unified School District Chinese Bilingual Department	San Francisco	336,226
	San Francisco Unified School District	San Francisco	180,500
	San Francisco Unified School District	San Francisco	153,537
	San Francisco Unified School District	San Francisco	212,800
	Alum Rock Union Elementary School District	San Jose	154,000
	Mt. Pleasant School District	San Jose	169,000
	San Jose Unified School District	San Jose	1,041,000
	San Leandro Unified School District	San Leandro	91,906
	San Ysidro School District	San Ysidro	100,000
	Santa Ana Unified School District	Santa Ana	230,250
	Santa Barbara County Schools Office of Superintendent	Santa Barbara	117,500
	Santa Barbara School District	Santa Barbara	150,500
	Santa Maria Joint Union School District	Santa Maria	178,373
	Santa Maria School District	Santa Maria	88,000
	Briggs-Olivelands Elementary Schools	Santa Paula	89,500
	Valle Lindo Elementary School District	South El Monte	144,000

Office of Bilingual Education Grant Awards, February 1975 (Continued)

STATE	LOCAL EDUCATION AGENCY (LEA)	CITY	AMOUNT
California (Continued)	South San Francisco Unified School District	South San Francisco	$ 70,000
	Stockton Unified School District	Stockton	472,775
	Coachella Valley Unified School District	Thermal	190,199
	New Haven Unified School District	Union City	175,480
	Pajaro Valley Unified School District	Watsonville	168,823
	Los Nietos Elementary School District	Whittier	116,000
	South Whittier School District	Whittier	120,937
	IHE's		
	College of Notre Dame	Belmont	25,200
	Cal State University–Fullerton	Fullerton	220,000
	Cal State University–Hayward	Hayward	100,000
	La Verne College	La Verne	42,800
	East Los Angeles College	Los Angeles	200,000
	Cal State University–Los Angeles	Los Angeles	300,000
	San Diego State University	San Diego	1,019,793
	San Diego City College	San Diego	50,000
	University of San Francisco	San Francisco	100,000
	University of the Pacific	Stockton	100,000
	Berkeley Unified School District *Materials Development Center*	Berkeley	593,283
	Berkeley Unified School District *Resource Center*	Berkeley	601,461
	California State Poly University Pomona Office of Teacher Preparation *Materials Development Center*	Pomona	717,320
COLORADO	Harrison School District No. 2	Colorado Springs	75,000
	Adams County School District No. 14	Commerce City	86,344
	Southwest Board of Coop. Services	Cortez	82,500
	Adams County School District No. 12	Denver	86,344
	Weld Board of Coop. Ed. Services	La Salle	87,000
	St. Vrain Valley School District–RE-1J	Longmont	51,000
	Huerfano School District	Walsenburg	81,000
CONNECTICUT	Bridgeport Board of Education	Bridgeport	137,200
	Hartford Board of Education	Hartford	241,890
	Consolidated School District of New Britain	New Britain	249,609
	Stamford Board of Education	Stamford	101,000
DELAWARE	Wilmington Board of Public Education	Wilmington	252,872
DISTRICT OF COLUMBIA	District of Columbia Public Schools	Washington, D.C.	175,007
FLORIDA	Ahfachkee Day School/BIA	Clewiston	29,398
	Pasco County School Board	Dade City	149,800
	Miccosukee Corporation	Miami	104,300
	The School Board of Dade County (Training)	Miami	248,068
	Collier County Public Schools	Naples	52,120
	The School Board of Dade County (Materials Development Center)	Miami	800,000
HAWAII	Hawaii State Department of Education	Honolulu	500,000
IDAHO	School District No. 131	Nampa	136,750
ILLINOIS	Chicago Board of Education	Chicago	2,661,077
	Chicago Consortium of Colleges and Universities	Chicago	115,000
	Northwest Educational Cooperative (Resource Center)	Mt. Prospect	637,493

Office of Bilingual Education Grant Awards, February 1975 (Continued)

STATE	LOCAL EDUCATION AGENCY (LEA)	CITY	AMOUNT
INDIANA	Hobart Township Community School	Hobart	$ 17,000
KANSAS	Finney County U.S.D. No. 457	Garden City	65,000
LOUISIANA	Tangipahoa Parish School Board	Amite	154,000
	Lafayette Parish School Board	Lafayette	128,000
	Iberia Parish School Board	New Iberia	136,000
	Orleans Parish School Board	New Orleans	214,000
	St. Landry Parish School Board	Opelousas	213,520
	St. Martin Parish School Board	St. Martinville	136,000
	Evangeline Parish School Board	Ville Platte	199,521
	Southeastern Louisiana University (IHE)	Hammond	40,000
	University of Southwestern Louisiana (Resource Center)	Lafayette	375,000
MAINE	Indian Township School Committee	Calais	114,000
	Caribou School Department	Caribou	108,996
	Maine School Administrative District No. 33 (St. John Valley Bilingual Program)	Frenchville	111,600
MASSACHUSETTS	Boston Public Schools	Boston	654,550
	Chelsea School Department	Chelsea	136,130
	Fall River Public Schools	Fall River	216,730
	Holyoke Public Schools	Holyoke	118,650
	Lawrence School Department	Lawrence	122,389
	New Bedford Public Schools	New Bedford	76,396
	Boston University (IHE)	Boston	150,000
	Fall River Public Schools (Dissemination Center)	Fall River	600,000
MICHIGAN	Detroit Public Schools	Detroit	110,000
	Grand Rapids Public Schools	Grand Rapids	337,000
	School District of the City of Pontiac (Training)	Pontiac	100,000
	Saginaw City School District	Saginaw	220,000
	Eastern Michigan University (IHE)	Ypsilanti	65,000
MINNESOTA	St. Paul Public Schools	St. Paul	185,000
MISSISSIPPI	BIA–Choctaw Board of Education	Philadelphia	311,746
	Mississippi State University (IHE)	Mississippi State	86,354
MISSOURI	School District of Kansas City	Kansas City	100,000
MONTANA	School District No. 87	Box Elder	101,000
	Hardin School District No. 17H	Hardin	155,046
	Lame Deer School District No. 6	Lame Deer	124,949
	Lodge Grass Elementary School District No. 27	Lodge Grass	50,254
	Wyola School District No. 29	Wyola	95,000
NEW HAMPSHIRE	Berlin School Department	Berlin	133,800
	The New Hampshire College and University Council (Resource Center)	Manchester	400,000
NEW JERSEY	Camden City Board of Education	Camden	360,000
	Lakewood Board of Education	Lakewood	398,321
	Long Branch Board of Education	Long Branch	162,784
	New Brunswick Board of Education	New Brunswick	212,600
	Board of Education City of Perth Amboy	Perth Amboy	186,493
	Trenton Board of Education	Trenton	311,121
	Union City Board of Education	Union City	167,425
	Vineland Board of Education	Vineland	151,437
	Woodstown-Pilesgrove Regional School District	Woodstown	123,905

Office of Bilingual Education Grant Awards, February 1975 (Continued)

STATE	LOCAL EDUCATION AGENCY (LEA)	CITY	AMOUNT
New Jersey (Continued)	Georgian Court College (IHE)	Lakewood	$ 11,340
	Rutgers University (IHE)	New Brunswick	150,000
	Kean College of New Jersey (IHE)	Union	53,582
NEW MEXICO	Albuquerque Public Schools	Albuquerque	200,000
	Central New Mexico Biling. Program Consortium (Training)	Albuquerque	60,000
	Bernalillo Public Schools	Bernalillo	173,000
	Clovis Municipal Schools	Clovis	102,000
	BIA Navajo Area Eastern Navajo Agency	Crownpoint	79,407
	Espanola Public Schools	Espanola	50,000
	Grants Municipal Schools	Grants	140,000
	Las Cruces School District No. 2	Las Cruces	124,000
	Las Vegas City Schools	Las Vegas	160,000
	West Las Vegas Schools	Las Vegas	180,000
	Ramah Navajo School Board., Inc.	Ramah	295,767
	Sky City Community School	San Fidel	137,592
	BIA North Pueblos Agency	Santa Fe	60,000
	Santa Fe Public Schools	Santa Fe	135,000
	Socorro Consolidated Schools	Socorro	120,000
	Taos Municipal Schools	Taos	126,000
	University of Albuquerque (IHE)	Albuquerque	45,000
	New Mexico Highlands University (IHE)	Las Vegas	200,000
	University of New Mexico	Albuquerque	470,000
	Ramah Navajo School Board., Inc. (Material Development Center)	Ramah	300,000
NEW YORK	Beacon Enlarged City School District	Beacon	187,913
	Brentwood Public Schools	Brentwood	107,350
	Buffalo Public School System	Buffalo	294,299
	Lawrence Public Schools	Cedarhurst	59,000
	Dunkirk Public Schools	Dunkirk	92,200
	N.Y.C. Board of Education-BCRMD	New York	232,860
	N.Y.C. Board of Education Project Best (Consortium)	New York	439,267
	N.Y.C. Board of Education-DSEPPS	New York	330,620
	N.Y.C. Board of Education Office of Bilingual Education	New York	239,500
	N.Y.C. Board of Education Office of High Schools Auxiliary Services	New York	299,652
	N.Y.C. Board of Education—C.S.D. No. 1	New York	334,606
	N.Y.C. Board of Education—C.S.D. No. 3	New York	309,545
	N.Y.C. Board of Education—C.S.D. No. 4	New York	327,510
	N.Y.C. Board of Education—C.S.D. No. 6	New York	310,844
	N.Y.C. Board of Education—C.S.D. No. 7	New York	164,707
	N.Y.C. Board of Education—C.S.D. No. 8	New York	298,200
	N.Y.C. Board of Education—C.S.D. No. 10	New York	236,500
	N.Y.C. Board of Education—C.S.D. No. 11	New York	271,919
	N.Y.C. Board of Education—C.S.D. No. 12	New York	290,065
	N.Y.C. Board of Education—C.S.D. No. 13	New York	311,300
	N.Y.C. Board of Education—C.S.D. No. 14	New York	308,679
	N.Y.C. Board of Education—C.S.D. No. 15	New York	333,972
	N.Y.C. Board of Education—C.S.D. No. 17	New York	295,500
	N.Y.C. Board of Education—C.S.D. No. 18	New York	306,830
	N.Y.C. Board of Education—C.S.D. No. 19	New York	368,042
	N.Y.C. Board of Education—C.S.D. No. 20	New York	311,770
	N.Y.C. Board of Education—C.S.D. No. 23	New York	287,546
	N.Y.C. Board of Education—C.S.D. No. 24	New York	312,400
	N.Y.C. Board of Education—C.S.D. No. 30	New York	250,000

Office of Bilingual Education Grant Awards, February 1975 (Continued)

STATE	LOCAL EDUCATION AGENCY (LEA)	CITY	AMOUNT
New York (Continued)	N.Y.C. Board of Education—C.S.D. No. 32	New York	$ 390,840
	N.Y.C. Board of Education—Louis Brandeis High School	New York	220,000
	N.Y.C. Board of Education, Bushwick High School	New York	148,028
	N.Y.C. Board of Education Eastern District High Schools	New York	217,500
	N.Y.C. Board of Education Fort Hamilton High School	New York	143,780
	N.Y.C. Board of Education Sarah Hale High School	New York	181,000
	N.Y.C. Board of Education John Jay High School	New York	223,240
	N.Y.C. Board of Education James Monroe High School	New York	192,400
	N.Y.C. Board of Education Newton High School	New York	199,500
	N.Y.C. Board of Education New Utrecht High School	New York	133,900
	N.Y.C. Board of Education Theodore Roosevelt High School	New York	204,000
	N.Y.C. Board of Education Seward Park High School	New York	218,460
	N.Y.C. Board of Education South Shore High School	New York	210,607
	N.Y.C. Board of Education Adlai Stevenson High School	New York	207,500
	N.Y.C. Board of Education George W. Wingate High School	New York	199,000
	Nyack Union Free School District	Nyack	84,600
	Sparkill Union Free School District	Sparkill	154,000
	North Rockland Central School District	Stony Point	229,000
	Little Flower U.F.S.D. at Wading River	Wading River	80,408
	Nassau Board of Coop. Educational Services	Westbury	391,500
	State University at Albany (IHE)	Albany	150,000
	Long Island University (IHE)	Brooklyn	150,000
	Hofstra University (IHE)	Hempstead	138,676
	Fordham University (IHE)	New York	86,116
	N.Y.C. Board of Education—C.S.B. No. 7 (Curriculum Development Center)	New York	483,000
	N.Y.C. Board of Education—Resource Center	New York	300,000
OKLAHOMA	Broken Bow Public Schools	Broken Bow	105,000
	Greasy School Board of Education	Stilwell	145,000
	Strother I.S.D. No. 14	Seminole	162,246
OREGON	Central School District	Independence	119,250
	Salem School District No. 24J	Salem	172,000
	Woodburn School District 103 C	Woodburn	212,000
PENNSYLVANIA	Allentown School District	Allentown	94,500
	Bristol Borough District No. 1	Bristol	107,800
	Harrisburg School District	Harrisburg	136,000
	Lancaster-Lebanon Intermediate Unit No. 13	Lancaster	334,643
	Reading School District	Reading	99,000
PUERTO RICO	Department of Education of Puerto Rico	Hato Rey, P.R.	556,100
RHODE ISLAND	Central Falls School Department	Central Falls	130,650

Office of Bilingual Education Grant Awards, February 1975 (Continued)

STATE	LOCAL EDUCATION AGENCY (LEA)	CITY	AMOUNT
Rhode Island (Continued)	East Providence School District	East Providence	$ 108,985
	Pawtucket School Department	Pawtucket	197,000
	Providence School Department	Providence	312,670
	Brown University (IHE)	Providence	61,894
	Rhode Island College (IHE)	Providence	86,792
	Providence School Department (Resource Center)	Providence	135,000
SOUTH DAKOTA	BIA Branch of Education, Loneman Day School, Pine Ridge Agency	Oglala	75,000
TEXAS	Abernathy I.S.D.	Abernathy	115,000
	Abilene I.S.D.	Abilene	120,000
	Alice I.S.D.	Alice	255,000
	Anthony I.S.D.	Anthony	325,000
	Austin I.S.D.	Austin	845,908
	Ed. Serv. Center Region XIII	Austin	165,000
	Bishop Consolidated I.S.D.	Bishop	85,000
	Brownsville I.S.D.	Brownsville	260,000
	Corpus Christi I.S.D.	Corpus Christi	155,000
	West Oso I.S.D.	Corpus Christi	195,000
	Crystal City I.S.D.	Crystal City	471,000
	Dallas I.S.D.	Dallas	468,344
	San Felipe-Del Rio C.I.S.D.	Del Rio	240,000
	Donna Independent School District	Donna	220,000
	Eagle Pass I.S.D.	Eagle Pass	178,176
	Edcouch-Elsa I.S.D.	Edcouch	215,000
	Edinburg Consolidated I.S.D.	Edinburg	215,000
	Region I Ed. Serv. Center	Edinburg	180,000
	Elgin I.S.D.	Elgin	110,000
	Region XIX Ed. Serv. Center	El Paso	90,000
	Yselta I.S.D.	El Paso	267,588
	Brooks County I.S.D.	Falfurrias	161,400
	Ft. Worth I.S.D.	Ft. Worth	445,332
	Galveston I.S.D.	Galveston	142,083
	Harlingen Consolidated I.S.D.	Harlingen	195,000
	Hereford I.S.D.	Hereford	85,000
	Houston I.S.D.	Houston	556,274
	Kingsville I.S.D.	Kingsville	250,000
	La Feria I.S.D.	La Feria	71,000
	La Joya I.S.D.	La Joya	150,000
	Laredo I.S.D.	Laredo	275,000
	United I.S.D.	Laredo	131,461
	La Villa I.S.D.	La Villa	125,000
	Levelland I.S.D.	Levelland	71,000
	Lubbock I.S.D.	Lubbock	131,758
	Lyford Consolidated I.S.D.	Lyford	117,004
	McAllen I.S.D.	McAllen	195,000
	Mercedes I.S.D.	Mercedes	190,000
	Mission Consolidated I.S.D.	Mission	190,000
	Pharr-San Juan-Alamo I.S.D.	Pharr	298,017
	Plainview I.S.D.	Plainview	117,542
	Port Isabel I.S.D.	Port Isabel	178,500
	Rio Grande City Consolidated I.S.D.	Rio Grande	210,965
	Rio Hondo I.S.D.	Rio Hondo	110,000
	Robstown I.S.D.	Robstown	305,000
	Lamar Consolidated I.S.D.	Rosenburg	120,000

Office of Bilingual Education Grant Awards, February 1975 (Continued)

STATE	LOCAL EDUCATION AGENCY (LEA)	CITY	AMOUNT
Texas (Continued)	Edgewood I.S.D.	San Antonio	$ 295,000
	Ed. Serv. Center Region 20	San Antonio	105,000
	Harlandale I.S.D.	San Antonio	295,000
	Northside I.S.D.	San Antonio	506,674
	San Antonio I.S.D.	San Antonio	548,795
	South San Antonio I.S.D.	San Antonio	135,000
	Southside I.S.D.	San Antonio	183,659
	San Diego I.S.D.	San Diego	180,000
	San Marcos Consolidated I.S.D.	San Marcos	110,000
	Waco I.S.D.	Waco	115,000
	Ed. Service Center Region XII	Waco	91,000
	Weslaco I.S.D.	Weslaco	198,000
	Region IX Ed. Serv. Center	Wichita Falls	110,000
	Zapata County I.S.D.	Zapata	182,777
	St. Edwards University (IHE)	Austin	60,000
	University of Texas at Austin (IHE)	Austin	140,000
	Pan American University (IHE)	Edinburg	125,000
	University of Texas at El Paso (IHE)	El Paso	140,000
	Texas A & I (IHE)	Kingsville	135,000
	Southwest Texas State University (IHE)	San Marcos	60,000
	Region XIII, Ed. Serv. Center (Dissemination & Assessment)	Austin	550,000
	Fort Worth I.S.D. (Materials Development Center)	Ft. Worth	707,000
	University of Texas at San Antonio (Dissemination & Assessment Center)	San Antonio	375,000
VERMONT	Essex-North Supervisory Union	Canaan	123,560
VIRGIN ISLANDS	Government of the Virgin Islands Charlotte Amalie	St. Thomas	253,250
WISCONSIN	Milwaukee Board of School Directors	Milwaukee	279,000
	University of Wisconsin (IHE)	Milwaukee	40,000
	Milwaukee Board of School Directors (Midwest Materials Development Center)	Milwaukee	245,000
WYOMING	Laramie County School District No. 1	Cheyenne	115,000
TRUST TERRITORIES OF THE PACIFIC ISLANDS	Kusaie Department of Education	Ponape District Eastern Caroline Islands	35,152
	Ponape Department of Education	Rolania Ponape Eastern Caroline Islands	68,952
	Headquarters of Education	Saipan Mariana Islands	52,813
	Marianas District Department of Education	Saipan Mariana Islands	129,915
	District Department of Education	Majuro Marshall Islands	78,086
	Truk Department of Education	Moen Island	65,165
	Palau Department of Education	Koror Palau Western Caroline Islands	84,868
	Yap District Department of Education	Colonia Yap	98,454

Source: Office of Bilingual Education. The Information has been rearranged specifically for this document.

APPENDIX C

Location of Lau Centers in the United States and the States Served

Area A—Institute for Urban and Minority Education, Teachers College, Columbia University, 525 120th St., New York, N.Y. 10027

> States—Connecticut, Maine, Massachusetts, New Hampshire, New Jersey, New York, Puerto Rico, Rhode Island, Vermont, Virgin Islands

Area B—University of Miami, School of Education, P.O. Box 8065, Coral Gables, Florida 33124

> States—Alabama, Delaware, Florida, Georgia, Kentucky, Maryland, Mississippi, North Carolina, Pennsylvania, South Carolina, Tennessee, Virginia, Washington, D.C., West Virginia

Area C—Chicago State University, 95th Street at King Drive, Chicago, Illinois 60628

> States—Illinois, Indiana, Iowa, Kansas, Michigan, Minnesota, Missouri, Nebraska, Ohio, Wisconsin

Area D—Intercultural Development Research Association, 114 Glenview W., Suite 118, San Antonio, Texas 78228

> States—Arkansas, Louisiana, Texas

Area E—Coalition of Indian Controlled School Boards, Suite 4, 811 Lincoln, Denver, Colorado 80203

> States—Colorado, Montana, North Dakota, Oklahoma, South Dakota, Utah, Wyoming

Area F—University of New Mexico, College of Education, Onate Hall, Room 223, Albuquerque, New Mexico 87131

> States—Arizona, Nevada, New Mexico

Area G—San Diego University, San Diego University Foundation, 5402 College Avenue, San Diego, California 92182

> States—That part of California south of the northern boundary of San Luis Obispo, Kern, and San Bernardino Counties

Area H—Berkeley Unified School District, 1414 Walnut Street, Berkeley, California 94709

> States—That part of California not included in Area G

Area I—Northwest Regional Educational Laboratory, Lindsay Building, 710 S.W. Second Avenue, Portland, Oregon 97204

> States—Alaska, Guam, Hawaii, Idaho, Oregon, Trust Territory of American Samoa, Washington

APPENDIX D

Major U.S. Commission on Civil Rights Hearings for Various
Linguistically and Culturally Distinct Peoples

Arizona (Window Rock)
Hearings Before the U.S. Commission on Civil Rights, October 22-24, 1973. (Transcript, not yet released.) Washington, D.C.: U.S. Commission on Civil Rights.

California
"Educational Neglect of the Mexican American in Lucia Mar Unified School District, Pismo Beach, California." A Report of the California State Advisory Committee to the U.S. Commission on Civil Rights. Washington, D.C.: U.S. Commission on Civil Rights, 1973.

"Education and the Mexican American Community in Los Angeles County." A Report of the California State Advisory Committee to the U.S. Commission on Civil Rights. Washington, D.C.: U.S. Commission on Civil Rights, April 1968.

"Asian Americans and Pacific Peoples: A Case of Mistaken Identity." (San Francisco) Washington, D.C.: U.S. Commission on Civil Rights, February 1975.

Illinois
"Bilingual Bicultural Education: A Right or Privilege?" A Report of the Illinois State Advisory Committee to the U.S. Commission on Civil Rights. Washington, D.C.: U.S. Commission on Civil Rights, 1974.

Massachusetts
"Issues of Concern to Puerto Ricans in Boston and Springfield, Massachusetts." A Report of the Massachusetts State Advisory Committee to the U.S. Commission on Civil Rights. Washington, D.C.: U.S. Commission on Civil Rights, 1972.

New York
Hearings Before the U.S. Commission on Civil Rights (Transcript), February 14-15, 1972, New York, New York. Washington, D.C.: U.S. Commission on Civil Rights.

Pennsylvania
"In Search of a Better Life: Education Problems of the Puerto Rican in Philadelphia, Pennsylvania." A Report of the Pennsylvania State Advisory Committee to the U.S. Commission on Civil Rights. Washington, D.C.: U.S. Commission on Civil Rights, 1974.

Texas (San Antonio)
"Hearings Before the U.S. Commission on Civil Rights, December 9-14, 1968." Washington, D.C.: U.S. Commission on Civil Rights, 1968.

Washington
"Indian Education in the State of Washington." A Report of the Washington State Advisory Committee to the U.S. Commission on Civil Rights. Washington, D.C.: U.S. Commission on Civil Rights, 1974.

APPENDIX E

Guidelines for the Preparation and Certification of Teachers
of Bilingual/Bicultural Education
(Center for Applied Linguistics, November 1974)

Personal Qualities

The teacher of bilingual/bicultural education should have the following qualifications:

1. A thorough knowledge of the philosophy and theory concerning bilingual/bicultural education and its application.

2. A genuine and sincere interest in the education of children regardless of their linguistic and cultural background, and personal qualities which contribute to success as a classroom teacher.

3. A thorough knowledge of and proficiency in the child's home language and the ability to teach content through it; an understanding of the nature of the language the child brings with him/her and the ability to utilize it as a positive tool in teaching.

4. Cultural awareness and sensitivity and a thorough knowledge of the cultures reflected in the two languages involved.

5. The proper professional and academic preparation obtained from a well-designed teacher training program in bilingual/bicultural education.

The guidelines which follow are designed to meet these necessary qualifications and describe the various academic areas considered essential in teacher training programs in bilingual/bicultural education.

I. Language Proficiency

The teacher should demonstrate the ability to:

1. Communicate effectively, both in speaking and understanding, in the languages and within the cultures of both home and school. The ability will include adequate control of pronunciation, grammar, vocabulary, and regional, stylistic, and nonverbal variants appropriate to the communication context.

2. Carry out instruction in all areas of the curriculum using a standard variety of both languages.

II. Linguistics

The teacher should demonstrate the ability to:

1. Recognize and accept the language variety of the home and a standard variety as valid systems of communication, each with its own legitimate functions.

2. Understand basic concepts regarding the nature of language.

3. Understand the nature of bilingualism and the process of becoming bilingual.

4. Understand basic concepts regarding the natural effects of contacts between languages and the implications of this information for the instructional program.

5. Identify and understand regional, social, and developmental varieties in the child's language(s) at the phonological, grammatical, and lexical levels.

6. Identify and understand structural differences between the child's first and second languages, recognizing areas of potential interference and positive transfer.

7. Develop curricular activities to deal with areas of interference.

8. Understand theories of first and second language learning, differences between child and adult language learning, and their implications for the classroom.

III. Culture

The teacher should demonstrate the ability to:

1. Respond positively to the diversity of behavior involved in cross-cultural environments.

2. Develop awareness in the learner of the value of cultural diversity.

3. Prepare and assist children to interact successfully in a cross-cultural setting.

4. Recognize and accept different patterns of child development within and between cultures in order to formulate realistic objectives.

5. Assist children to maintain and extend identification with and pride in the mother culture.

6. Understand, appreciate and incorporate into activities, materials and other aspects of the instructional environment:

   a. The culture and history of the group's ancestry.
   b. Contributions of group to history and culture of the United States.
   c. Contemporary life style(s) of the group.

7. Recognize both the similarities and differences between Anglo-American and other cultures and both the potential conflicts and opportunities they may create for children.

8. Know the effects of cultural and socioeconomic variables on the student's learning styles (cognitive and affective) and on the student's general level of development and socialization.

9. Use current research regarding the education of children in the U.S. from diverse linguistic and cultural backgrounds.

10. Understand the effects of socioeconomic and cultural factors on the learner and the educational program.

11. Recognize differences in social structure, including familial organizations and patterns of authority, and their significance for the program.

IV. Instructional Methods

This component should enable teachers to assist students in achieving their full academic potential in the home language and culture as well as in English. To this end, the teacher is expected to demonstrate the following competencies:

1. Assist children to maintain and extend command of the mother tongue and the second language in listening, speaking, reading, and writing.

2. Apply teaching strategies appropriate to distinct learning modes and developmental levels, including preschool, taking into consideration how differences in culture affect these and other learning variables.

3. Organize, plan, and teach specific lessons in the required curriculum areas, using the appropriate terminology in the learner's language(s) and observing the local district curriculum guidelines. Basic elements and methodologies best suited to the teaching of reading and language arts, mathematics, social studies, and science, as a minimum, must be identified and applied in the learner's language(s).

4. Utilize innovative techniques effectively and appropriately in the learner's language(s) in the various content areas, namely:

    a. Formulation of realistic performance objectives and their assessment.

    b. Inquiry/discovery strategies.

    c. Individualized instruction.

    d. Learning centers.

    e. Uses of media and audiovisual materials.

    f. Systems approaches to the teaching of reading and mathematics skills.

    g. Team teaching and cross grouping.

    h. Interaction analysis.

5. Develop an awareness of the way in which the learner's culture should permeate significant areas of the curriculum.

6. Utilize first and/or second-language techniques in accordance with the learner's needs at various stages of the learning process.

7. Utilize effective classroom management techniques, for optimal learning in specific situations.

8. Work effectively with paraprofessionals and other adults.

9. Identify and utilize available community resources in and outside the classroom.

V. Curriculum Utilization and Adaptation

The teacher should demonstrate the ability to:

1. Identify current biases and deficiencies in existing curriculum and in both commercial and teacher-prepared materials of instruction. Materials should be evaluated in accordance with the following criteria:

    a. Suitability to student's language proficiencies and cultural experiences.

    b. Provisions and respect for linguistic and cultural diversity.

    c. Objectives, scope, and sequence of the materials in terms of content areas.

    d. Student's reaction to materials.

2. Acquire, evaluate, adapt, and develop materials appropriate to the bilingual/bicultural classroom.

VI. Assessment

General. The teacher should demonstrate the ability to:

1. Recognize potential linguistic and cultural biases of existing assessment instruments and procedures when prescribing a program for the learner.

2. Utilize continuous assessment as part of the learning process.

3. Interpret diagnostic data for the purpose of prescribing instructional programs for the individual.

4. Use assessment data as basis for program planning and implementation.

Language. The teacher should demonstrate the ability to:

1. Determine language dominance of the learner in various domains of language use—oral and written.

2. Use assessment results to determine teaching strategies for each learner.

3. Identify areas of proficiency (oral and written: vocabulary, syntax, phonology) in the learner's first and second language.

4. Assess maintenance and extension levels of the learner's language(s).

Content. The teacher should demonstrate the ability to:

1. Evaluate growth, using teacher-prepared as well as standard instruments, in cognitive skills and knowledge of content areas utilizing the language of the home.

2. Assess accuracy and relevance of materials utilized in the classroom.

3. Prepare tests to evaluate achievement of proposed objectives of instruction.

Self. The teacher should demonstrate the ability to identify and apply procedures for the assessment of:

1. Own strengths and weaknesses as a bilingual teacher.

2. Own value system as it relates to the learner, his/her behavior, and his/her background.

3. The effectiveness of own teaching strategies.

VII. School-Community Relations

Current trends in education have specifically identified the significant role of the community in the educational process. The knowledge that the community has goals and expectations creates for the schools the need to include, integrate, and enhance those expectations in the regular school program.

Bilingual education offers distinct opportunities to bridge the structural and cultural gap between school and community. The school with a bilingual/bicultural education program should serve as a catalyst for the integration of diverse cultures within the community.

The teacher should demonstrate the following competencies:

1. Develop basic awareness concerning the importance of parental and community involvement for facilitating learners' successful integration to their school environment.

2. Acquire skills to facilitate basic contacts and interaction between a learner's family and school personnel.

3. Demonstrate leadership in establishing home/community exchange of sociocultural information which can enrich the learner's instructional activities.

4. Acquire and develop skills in collecting culturally relevant information and materials characteristic of both the historical and current life-styles of the learners' culture(s) that can serve both for curriculum content and for instructional activities.

5. Acquire a knowledge of the patterns of child rearing represented in the families of the learners so as to better understand the background of the learners' behaviors in the classroom.

6. To act as facilitator for enhancing the parents' roles, functions, and responsibilities in the school and community.

7. Serve as a facilitator for the exchange of information and views concerning the rationale, goals, and procedures for the instructional programs of the school.

8. To plan for and provide the direct participation of a learner's family in the regular instructional programs and activities.

VIII. Supervised Teaching

Because of the great disparity between theory presented in the context of a college environment and practical teaching realities in a bilingual/bicultural classroom setting, it is essential that a portion of every teacher's training include on-site supervised teaching experience in a bilingual/bicultural program. To the extent possible, relevant competencies should be demonstrated in the direct context of such a classroom setting.

APPENDIX F

RANDOM SAMPLE OF HIGHER EDUCATION INSTITUTIONS IN THE SOUTHWEST THAT HAVE TEACHER EDUCATION PROGRAMS

State	Institution	Total professional staff of schools of education	Spanish-surnamed professional staff members of schools of education
CALIFORNIA	California College of Arts and Crafts	11	1
	California Polytechnic State University, San Luis Obispo	19	
	California State College, San Bernardino	13	2
	California State University, Fullerton	83	0
	California State University, Hayward	94	3
	California State University, Los Angeles	145	8
	Dominican College	5	0
	Monterey Institute of Foreign Studies	14	0
	San Diego State University	144	3
	Stanford University	78	3
	University of California, Riverside	23	1
	Westmont College	7	0
	San Jose State University	95	2
COLORADO	Colorado College	28	0
	Metropolitan State College	16	1
	Southern Colorado State College	17	4
NEW MEXICO	Eastern New Mexico University	27	0
	New Mexico Highlands University	16	4
TEXAS	Abilene Christian College	16	0
	Angelo State University	11	0
	Dallas Baptist College	6	0
	Lubbock Christian College	6	0
	McMurry College	6	1
	Stephen F. Austin University	40	0
	Tarleton State College	12	0
	West Texas State University	27	0
	TOTAL	959	33

Source: U.S. Commission on Civil Rights, College Catalogue Review, February 1973. The information has been rearranged specifically for this document.

APPENDIX G

BIBLIOGRAPHY OF ERIC PUBLICATIONS

("ED" numbers are ERIC document identifications. Journal articles are listed in ERIC's *Current Index to Journals in Education.*)

Abeytia, Hector, and others. "Agencies and the Migrant: Theory and Reality of the Migrant Condition. First Papers on Migrancy and Rural Poverty: An Introduction to the Education of Mexican-Americans in Rural Areas." Los Angeles: School of Education, University of Southern California, 1968. ED 026173

Adams, Raymond S., and others. "Sociology and the Training of Teachers of the Disadvantaged: A Final Report, Part II." Columbia: College of Education, University of Missouri, 1970. ED 050301

Adkins, Dorothy C., and Crowelle, Doris C. "Field Test of the University of Hawaii Preschool Language Curriculum. Final Report." Honolulu: Educational Research and Development Center, University of Hawaii, 1970. ED 048924

Adler, Elaine F. "Basic Concerns of Teaching English as a Second Language in New Jersey." Speech delivered at the meeting of the Foreign Language Teachers Association, New Jersey Education Association, November 7, 1968. ED 034194

Ainsworth, C. L., editor. "Teachers and Counselors for Mexican American Children." Austin, Texas: Southwest Educational Development Laboratory, 1969. ED 029728

American Association of Colleges for Teacher Education. "Excellence in Teacher Education: 1971 Distinguished Achievement Awards Programs." Washington, D.C.: the Association, 1971. ED 051095

_____. "Excellence in Teacher Education: 1969 Distinguished Achievement Awards of the American Association of Colleges for Teacher Education." Washington, D.C.: the Association, 1969. ED 026347

Anderson, John. "The New School and Indian Communities." *Northian* 8: 28-31; Spring 1971.

Arizona State University. "New Horizons for Indian Education." Ninth Annual American Indian Education Conference, March 22-23, 1968. Tempe: Indian Education Center, Arizona State University, 1968.

Ayala, Armando A. "Rationale for Early Childhood Bilingual-Bicultural Education." Paper presented at the annual convention of the American Educational Research Association, New York, February 1971. ED 047869

Barnett, Don C., and Aldous, Myrtle. "Ten Principles Underlying a Teacher Education Program for Native People." *Northian* 9: 36-38; Spring 1973.

Barnhardt, Ray. "Being a Native and Becoming a Teacher in the Alaska Rural Teacher Training Corps." Paper presented at the annual meeting of the American Anthropological Association, New Orleans, 1973. ED 088631

Bartley, Diana E. "Soviet Approaches to Bilingual Education. Language and the Teacher: A Series in Applied Linguistics, Vol. 10." Philadelphia: Center for Curriculum Development, 1971. ED 055505

Bauch, Jerold P. "Community Participation in Teacher Education: Teacher Corps and the Model Programs." GEM Bulletin 70-4. Athens: College of Education, University of Georgia, 1970. ED 042700

Bauer, E. W. "The Migrant Child and his Psycho-Linguistic Problems." Paper presented at a conference on "The Migrant Child and the School," Melbourne, Australia, August 30, 1971. ED 058775

Beck, John M., and Black, Timuel. "National Teacher Corps, Second Cycle Report, 1967-1969." Chicago: Chicago Consortium of Colleges and Universities, 1969. ED 041824

Bell, Paul W. "Bilingual Education—A Second Look." *TESOL Newsletter* 5: 29-30; September-December 1971.

Bernal, Ernest M. Jr., editor. "The San Antonio Conference: Bilingual-Bicultural Education—Where Do We Go from Here? (San Antonio, Texas, March 28-29, 1969)." San Antonio: St. Mary's University, March 1969. ED 033777

Bertolaet, Frederick, and Usdan, Michael. "Development of School-University Programs for the Preservice Education of Teachers for the Disadvantaged Through Teacher Education Centers." Chicago: Great Cities Research Council, 1965. ED 002463

Blair, George E., and others. "Teaching Ethnic Groups," April 1967. ED 012735

Blanco, George. "Texas Report on Education for Bilingual Students," November 1967. ED 017388

Born, Warren C., editor. "Papers Presented at the Annual Meeting of the New York State Association of Foreign Language Teachers (55th, Kiamescha Lake, New York, October 9-11, 1972)." New York State Association of Foreign Language Teachers, 1973. ED 086022

Barcy, Maryruth, editor. "Workpapers in Teaching English as a Second Language, Vol. IV." Los Angeles: University of California, 1970. ED 054664

Brandt, Dorothy Pauline. "The Development and Evaluation of an In-Service Program in Social Studies and Science for First-Grade Teachers." Austin: University of Texas, 1967. ED 027199

Braxton, Edward, and others. "High Roads Project." New York: Ford Foundation, 1960. ED 001929

Breivogel, William F., and others. "The Florida Parent Education Model as an Agent of Change." Washington, D.C.: American Psychological Association, September 1970. ED 043061

Brod, Richard I. "A National Foreign Language Program for the 1970's." New York: Modern Language Association of America, June 1973. ED 098820

Burger, Henry G. "Ethno-Pedagogy: A Manual in Cultural Sensitivity, with Techniques for Improving Cross-Cultural Teaching by Fitting Ethnic Patterns." Second Edition. Albuquerque: Southwestern Cooperative Educational Laboratory, August 1968. ED 024653

Byrd, Suzanne. "Bilingual Education: Report on the International Bilingual Bicultural Conference." *Bulletin of the Association of Departments of Foreign Languages* 6: 39-41; September 1974.

California State College. "Operation Fair Chance: The Establishment of Two Centers To Improve the Preparation of Teachers of Culturally Disadvantaged Students, Emphasizing Occupational Understanding Leading to Technical-Vocational Competence. Final Report." Hayward: the College, September 1969. ED 035710

California State Department of Education, Office of Compensatory Education. "California Plan for the Education of Migrant Children, Evaluation Report, July 1, 1967-June 30, 1968." Sacramento: the Department, 1968. ED 028009

————. "Minutes and Proceedings of the Conference of the California Council on the Education of Teachers (Santa Barbara, March 30-April 1, 1967)." Sacramento: the Department, April 1967. ED 014452

Carter, Thomas P. "Preparing Teachers for Mexican American Children." Paper prepared for the Conference on Teacher Education for Mexican Americans, New Mexico State University, Las Cruces, New Mexico, February 13-15, 1969. ED 025367

Casso, Henry J. "The Siesta Is Over." Paper delivered at the conference on "Improving the Preparation of Educational Personnel To Serve in School Systems Enrolling a Significant Number of Mexican American Students," New Mexico State University, February 13-15, 1969. ED 034199

Castaneda, A. "Persisting Ideologies of Assimilation in America: Implications for Psychology and Education." *ATISBOS: Journal of Chicano Research*, Summer 1975. pp. 79-91.

Castillo, Max S., and Cruz, Josue Jr., "Special Competencies for Teachers of Preschool Chicano Children: Rationale, Content and Assessment Process." *Young Children* 29: 341-47; September 1974.

Cavender, Chris C. "Suggested Educational Programs for Teachers and Parents of Urban Indian Youth." Minneapolis: Center for Urban and Regional Affairs, Training Center for Community Programs, October 1971. ED 057969

Center for Applied Linguistics. "Guidelines for the Preparation and Certification of Teachers of Bilingual/Bicultural Education." Arlington, Va.: the Center, November 1974. ED 098809

Center for the Study of Migrant and Indian Education. "Student Teaching and Related Experiences." Toppenish, Wash.: the Center, June 1970. ED 046889

Chandler, B. J., and others. "Research Seminar on Teacher Education." Evanston, Ill.: Northwestern University, 1963. ED 003428

Chavez, Rafael, editor. "National Conference: Early Childhood Education and the Chicanito (Tucson, Arizona, August 3-5, 1972)." Tucson: Pima Community College, 1972. ED 082819

Chazan, Maurice, editor. *Compensatory Education.* London: Butterworth and Co., 1973. ED 074179

Chicago Public Schools. "De todo Un Poco (A Little of Everything)." Chicago: the Schools, May 1972. ED 066972

Christensen, Rosemary, and others. "Native American Teacher Corps Conference (Denver, Colorado, April 26-29, 1973). Position Papers, Vol. 2." Billings: Eastern Montana College, 1973. ED 078994

Comptroller General of the United States. "Assessment at Northern Arizona University and Participating Schools on the Navajo and Hopi Indian Reservations." Washington, D.C.: the Comptroller General, 1971. ED 053100

Condon, Elaine C., and others. "Project Sell, Title VII: Final Evaluation 1970-1971." Union City, N.J.: Board of Education, 1971. ED 067951

Coombs, L. Madison. "The Educational Disadvantage of the Indian American Student." University Park: New Mexico State University, July 1970. ED 040815

Crisp, Raymond D., and others. "KWIC-Index Bibliography of Selected References on the Preparation of Secondary School English Teachers." Urbana: Illinois State-Wide Curriculum Study Center in the Preparation of Secondary English Teachers, July 1969. ED 031488

Cudecki, Edwin. "Report of a Three-Week Study Tour of the Federal Republic of Germany and Its Educational System." Chicago: Department of Curriculum, Board of Education, December 1971. ED 074850

DeBeer, A. G. "The Teaching of English as a Second Language in Afrikaans High Schools." Pretoria: English Academy of Southern Africa, 1967. ED 027543

Denver Board of Education. "A Project for Educational Opportunities Through Enriched and Improved Education Programs. ESEA Title 1 Evaluation Report, 1967-1968." Denver: Board of Education, School District No. 1, 1968. ED 038455

Derrick, June. "The Language Needs of Immigrant Children." *London Educational Review* 2: 25-30; Spring 1973.

Detrich, Daniel J., compiler. "Annotated Bibiliography of Research in the Teaching of English, January 1, 1974, to June 30, 1974." Urbana, Ill.: ERIC Clearinghouse on Reading and Communication Skills, 1974. ED 095556

Ditchley Foundation (Oxford, England). "Education for the Less Privileged: A Report of the Anglo American Conference on Education for the Less Privileged." Dayton, Ohio: Institute for Development of Educational Activities, 1970. ED 045794

Dodd, William J. "Address to the Opening General Session, Fifth Annual TESOL Convention, New Orleans, March 4, 1971." ED 053600

Dalvi, Kunda. "Teaching the Deaf in India." *Volta Review* 72: 272-77; May 1970.

Dominguez, Fernando. "Bilingual Education: A Needs Assessment Case Study." Teacher Corps Associates, Resources for CBTE, No. 5. Santa Cruz: University of California, 1973. ED 095148

Doyle, Michael. "Language Arts and Migrant Education in Michigan." *Education* 92: 107-109; November-December 1971.

Dozier, Edward P. "The Teacher and the Indian Student." *Freedomways* 9: 328-33; February 1969.

Dugas, Donald G. "Facilitating the Self-Actualization of Franco-Americans." Paper presented at the Fifth Annual TESOL Meeting, New Orleans, March 1971. ED 055482

Dunfee, Maxine. "Ethnic Modification of the Curriculum." Report of a Conference on Ethnic Modification of the Curriculum, St. Louis, Missouri, November 20-22, 1969. ED 062469

Dykes, Archie R. "Training Institute for Staff Members of School Systems with Multi-Cultural Schools." Memphis, Tenn.: Center for Advanced Graduate Study in Education, Memphis State University, 1966. ED 073058

Eland, Calvin. "The Culturally Disadvantaged: A Field Experience Guide. Materials/One." Washington, D.C.: American Association of Colleges for Teacher Education, 1968. ED 080497

Elefant, William L., editor. "Israel Education Abstracts. A Selected Bibliography of Current and Past Literature and Materials on the Philosophy, Policy and Practice of Education in Israel." Jerusalem: Israel Program for Scientific Translation, November 1970. ED 049139

Escondido Union School District. "Cycle II Teacher Corps. Joint Proposal-Final Report." Escondido, Calif.: the District, 1969. ED 041825

Esquibel, Antonio A. "Southern Colorado State College Teacher Corps." Pueblo: Southern Colorado State College, 1972. ED 084247

Ether, John A. "Preparing the Teacher of English for the Inner City." Oswego: New York State English Council, October 1969. ED 035647

_____. "Teacher Preparation for the Minority and Disadvantaged." NCRIEEO Tipsheet, No. 10. New York: National Center for Research and Information on Equal Educational Opportunity, Columbia University, 1973. ED 073224

Evertts, Eldonna L., editor. "Dimensions of Dialect." Champaign, Ill.: National Council of Teachers of English, 1967. ED 030623

Faas, Larry A. "A Career Development Program for Indian Teachers." *Journal of American Indian Education* 11: 13-14; January 1972.

Fallon, Berlie J., editor. "40 Innovative Programs in Early Childhood Education." Belmont, Calif.: Lear Siegler, 1973. ED 093468

Ferguson, Edward T., and Bice, Gary R., editors. "Annual National Vocational-Technical Teacher Education Seminar Proceedings, Teaching Disadvantaged Youth (Third, Miami Beach, Florida, October 20-23, 1969), Final Report." Leadership Series No. 24. Columbus:

Center for Vocational and Technical Education, Ohio State University, June 1969. ED 037540

Field, Ralph G., and Miller, Larry E. "Training Teachers for the Disadvantaged Through Apprenticeship Programs." *Agricultural Education Magazine* 45: 88-91; October 1972.

Finocchiaro, Mary. "Teaching English to Speakers of Other Languages: Problems and Priorities." Special Anthology Issue and Monograph 14, adapted from an address presented to the New York TESOL Affiliate, New York City, November 11, 1970. Oswego: New York State English Council, 1971. ED 053604

Fisher, John C. "Bilingualism in Puerto Rico: A History of Frustration." Oswego: New York State English Council, April 1971. ED 053608

Freeman, Larry. "The Impact of Legal Decisions on the Future of Education." Washington, D.C.: ERIC Clearinghouse on Teacher Education, 1974. ED 097291

Frost, Joe L., and Rowland, G. Thomas. *Compensatory Programming: The Acid Test of American Education.* Dubuque, Iowa: William C. Brown Co., 1971. ED 066529

Galarza, Ernesto, and Samora, Julian. "Chicano Studies: Research and Scholarly Activity." *Civil Rights Digest* 3: 40-42; February 1970.

Garcia, Ernest F. "Chicano Cultural Diversity: Implications for CBTE," May 1974. ED 091375

Gillam, Marshall R. "American Indians as Student Teachers." Paper prepared for Section Meeting on Directions in American Education, National Council for the Social Studies, San Francisco, November 1973. ED 092298

Girad, Ghislaine. "Man in the North Technical Paper. Education in the Canadian North. Report Three: Southern Teachers for the North." Montreal: Arctic Institute of North America, 1973. ED 077622

_____. "Training of Native Teachers in Quebec." Speech prepared for the International Conference on Cross-Cultural Education, Montreal, August 18-21, 1969. ED 092275

Golub, Lester S. "Computer Assisted Instruction in English Teacher Education." Paper presented at the Conference on English Education, National Council of Teachers of English, St. Louis, April 1972. ED 064277.

Goodman, Frank M. "Compton Bilingual Plan Review Report 1971-72." Compton, Calif.: Compton Unified School District, 1972. ED 072676

Graham, Richard, and others. "The Mexican-American Heritage: Developing Understanding. First Papers on Migrancy and Rural Poverty: An Introduction to the Education of Mexican Americans in Rural Areas." Los Angeles: School of Education, University of Southern California, 1968. ED 026174

Gray, Susan W., and others. "Research, Change, and Social Responsibility: An Illustrative Model from Early Education." Nashville, Tenn.: Demonstration and Research Center for Early Education, George Peabody College for Teachers, September 1967. ED 032922

Griffin, Robert J. "Tenes Anyone?" *American Foreign Language Teacher* 3: 27-28; Spring 1973.

Guernsey, John. "Rise and Shine." *American Education* 5: 20-21; November 1969.

Guerra, Emilio L. "Training Teachers for Spanish-Speaking Children on the Mainland." Address delivered at the Conference on the Education of Puerto Rican Children on the Mainland, San Juan, October 18-21, 1970. ED 046300

Haizlip, Harold. "Speech to Faculty of Harvard-Boston Summer Program at Preplanning Meeting," March 1965. ED 001507

Harrison, G. Scott. "Some Cultural and Linguistic Background Information for a Beginning Teacher on the Navajo Reservation." Master of Arts Independent Study Project, School for International Training of the Experiment in International Living, 1971. ED 071505

Harrison, Helene W. "Final Evaluation Report of the Harlandale Independent School District Bilingual Education Program." San Antonio, Texas: Harlandale Independent School District, 1974. ED 091108

Harstead, Pat, and Venner, Herb. "Project To Utilize Volunteers in Eliminating Adult Illiteracy. Quarterly Progress Report, First Quarter." Washington, D.C.: U.S. Department of Health, Education, and Welfare, 1970. ED 047238

Harthshorne, K. B. "The Teaching of English in Bantu Schools in South Africa: Some Comments on the Present Situation." Pretoria: English Academy of Southern Africa, 1967. ED 027544

Haubrich, Vernon F. "Federal Funds and Teacher Education," 1966. ED 012699

Hawkins, James E. "Indian Education in the Bureau of Indian Affairs." Washington, D.C.: Bureau of Indian Affairs, U.S. Department of the Interior, November 1972. ED 075130

Henrie, Samuel N., editor. "A Sourcebook of Elementary Curricula Programs and Projects." San Francisco: Far West Laboratory for Educational Research and Development, 1974. ED 098734

Henry, David D. "The Latin American Scholarship Program of American Universities." *International Educational and Cultural Exchange* 7: 30-55; Winter 1972.

Hernandez, Alberto, and Melnick, Susan L. "Modular Sequence: English as a Second Language, Methods and Techniques. TTP 001.14. Teaching ESL in Context. Teacher Corps Bilingual Project." West Hartford, Conn.: College of Education, University of Hartford, n.d. ED 095142

———. "Modular Sequence: English as a Second Language, Methods and Techniques. TTP 001.01. TESOL Overview. Teacher Corps Bilingual Project." West Hartford, Conn.: College of Education, University of Hartford, n.d. ED 095129

———. "Modular Sequence: English as a Second Language, Methods and Techniques. Instructor's Guide. Teacher Corps Bilingual Project." West Hartford, Conn.: College of Education, University of Hartford, n.d. ED 095128

Hess, Richard T. "Content Analysis Schedule for Bilingual Education Programs: Cherokee Bilingual Education Program." New York: Hunter College Bilingual Education Applied Research Unit, City University of New York, 1972. ED 072704

Heywood, Stanley J., and others. "Native American Teacher Corps Conference (Denver, Colorado, April 26-29, 1973), Position Papers, Vol. 1." Billings: Eastern Montana College, 1973. ED 078993.

Hillson, Maurie, and others. *Education and the Urban Community: Schools and the Crisis of the Cities.* New York: American Book Co., 1969. ED 040233

Hoboken Board of Education. "Assimilation thru Cultural Understanding. ESEA Title III— Phase III. Part II: Narrative Report; Application for Continuation Grant. Part III: Projected Activities. Attachments." Hoboken, N.J.: the Board, 1969. ED 033185

Holland, Thomas R., and Lee, Catherine M., editors. "The Alternative of Radicalism: Radical and Conservative Possibilities for Teaching the Teachers of America's Young Children." Proceedings of the Fifth National Conference of the Tri-University Project, New Orleans, January 29-31, 1969. Lincoln: University of Nebraska, 1969. ED 046941

Hopkins, Thomas R. "American Indians and the English Language Arts." *Florida Foreign Language Reporter* 7: 145-46; Spring-Summer 1969.

Hughes, B. E., and Harrison, Helene W. "Evaluation Report of the Bilingual Education Program: Harlandale Independent School District, San Marcos Independent School District, Southwest Texas State University, 1970-1971." San Antonio: Harlandale Independent School District, 1971. ED 055686

Hughes, Marie M. "Community Components in Teacher Education." Storrs: National Leadership Institute—Teacher Education/Early Childhood, University of Connecticut, November 1971. ED 084248

Hunter, William, editor. "Multicultural Education Through Competency-Based Teacher Education." Washington, D.C.: American Association of Colleges for Teacher Education, 1974. ED 098226

Hutasoit, Marnixius, and Porter, Clifford H. "A Study of the 'New Primary Approach' in the Schools of Kenya." Nairobi: Ministry of Education, March 1965. ED 025738

Jablonsky, Adelaide, and others. "Imperatives for Change." Proceedings of the New York State Education Conference on College and University Programs for Teachers of the Disadvantaged, Yeshiva University, April 10-11, 1967. Albany: New York State Education Department, 1967. ED 018454

Jackson, Virginialee D. "A Descriptive Study of Teacher Education Programs for Navajo Indian College Students," 1974. ED 092296

James, Charles J., compiler. "A Selective Bibliography of Doctoral Dissertations in Modern Language Education." New York: ERIC Clearinghouse on Languages and Linguistics, 1972. ED 069187

John, Vera P., and Horner, Vivian M. *Early Childhood Bilingual Education.* New York: Modern Language Association of America, 1971. ED 047593

Jones, Donald W., editor. "Human Relations in Teacher Education." Muncie, Ind.: Ball State University, August 1970. ED 055965

Jones, Earl, and others. "An Evaluation Report on the Regional Educational Agencies Project (Alabama, Louisiana, Tennessee, Texas) in International Education." Austin: Office of International and Bilingual Education, Texas Education Agency, July 1970. ED 048086

Julien, Daniel J., and Monsma, John W. "Teaching Communication to Indian Educators." Paper presented at the International Communications Association Annual Convention, Atlanta, Georgia, April 1972. ED 064925

Kalectaca, Milo. "Competencies for a Hopi Reservation Teacher. Hopi Background Competencies for Teachers." Teacher Corps Associates: Resources for CBTE, No. 7. Flagstaff: Northern Arizona University, 1973. ED 095952

————. "Competencies for Teachers of Culturally Different Children. Teacher Competencies for Teaching Native American Children." Paper prepared for Writing Conference on Multicultural Education, CBE Teacher Competencies Effective with Youth from Different Cultural Groups, June 1974. ED 091379

Kaltsounis, Theodore. "The Indian Teacher Education Program at the University of Washington." *College of Education Record* (University of Washington) 37: 68-70; May 1971.

Kaniel, Soshana. "The Social Background of Students and Their Prospect of Success at School." Israel National Commission for UNESCO, May 1971. ED 060274.

Kaplan, Leonard, and Tocco, T. Salvatore. "Impact of the Florida Model Follow Through Program on a Sponsoring Institution." Paper presented at the American Psychological Association Meeting, Miami, September 1970. ED 045563

Karnes, Merle B. "A New Role for Teachers: Involving the Entire Family in the Education of Preschool Disadvantaged Children." Urbana: Institute of Research for Exceptional Children, University of Illinois, 1969. ED 036339

Karr, Ken, and McGuire, Esther. "Mexican Americans on the Move—Are Teacher Preparation Programs in Higher Education Ready?" 1969. ED 031348

Kersey, Harry A., Jr. "Training Teachers in a Seminole Indian School—A Unique Experience with the Disadvantaged Child." *Journal of Teacher Education* 22: 25-28; Spring 1971.

Kleinfeld, Judith. "Preparing Teachers for the Cross-Cultural Classroom," 1974. ED 094920

Klingstedt, Joe Lars. "Teachers of Middle School Mexican American Children: Indicators of Effectiveness and Implications for Teacher Education," 1972. ED 059828

Kniefle, Tanya Suarez, compiler. "Programs Available for Strengthening the Education of Spanish-Speaking Students." Paper prepared for the Conference on Teacher Education for Mexican Americans, New Mexico State University, February 13-15, 1969. ED 025366

Kreidler, Carol J., editor. "On Teaching English to Speakers of Other Languages, Series II." Papers read at the TESOL Conference, San Diego, California, March 12-13, 1965. Champaign, Ill.: National Council of Teachers of English, 1966. ED 034202

La Fontaine, Hernan. "The Bilingual School (P.S. 25, Bronx)." Brooklyn: New York City Board of Education, May 1970. ED 066983

Landes, Ruth. *Culture in American Education: Anthropological Approaches to Minority and Dominant Groups in the Schools.* New York: John Wiley and Sons, 1965. ED 012285

Lange, Dale L., and James, Charles J., editors. "Foreign Language Education: A Reappraisal." New York: American Council on the Teaching of Foreign Languages, 1972. ED 073717

————. "1972 ACTFL Annual Bibliography of Books and Articles on Pedagogy in Foreign Language." *Foreign Language Annals* 6: 537-658; May 1973.

"Le Milieu Social des Eleves et Leur Chances de Succes a l'Ecole (The Social Background of Students and Their Chance of Success at School," September 1971. ED 060278

Lesley, Tay. "Bilingual Education in California." Master's thesis. Los Angeles: University of California, 1971. (Unpublished) ED 057661

Lewis, Horacio D. "To Train or Not To Train Teachers for Spanish-Speaking Communities." *Viewpoints* 49: 15-29; July 1973.

Leyba, Charles. "A Brief Bibliography on Teacher Education and Chicanos." Washington, D.C.: ERIC Clearinghouse on Teacher Education, 1974. ED 090147

Lezama, Juan A. "Bilingualism, the Mexican American College Student, and His Community." Paper presented at the Fifth Annual TESOL Convention, New Orleans, March 1971. ED 066935

Library of Congress. "Language and Area Studies Programs and the Participation of Spanish and Portuguese Speaking Minorities in American Society." Report of a meeting held at Miami, Florida, May 1-3, 1969. ED 036599

Lickona, Thomas, and others. "Excellence in Teacher Education." *Today's Education* 62: 89-94; September-October 1973.

Light, Richard L. "Issues in Teacher Preparation for Cross-Cultural Education." Paper presented at the International Conference on Bilingual Bicultural Education, New York, 1974. ED 093181

————. "On Language Arts and Minority Children." Speech given at the annual convention of the National Council of Teachers of English, Washington, D.C., November 1969. ED 040195

Lindberg, Dormalee H., and Swick, Kevin J. "Developing Creative Materials for Teaching the Culturally Different Child." Paper presented at the annual meeting of the Association of Teacher Educators, Chicago, February 23, 1973. ED 090159

Linton, Marigold. "Problems of Indian Children." Paper presented at the American Psychological Association Convention in Miami Beach, Florida, September 3-8, 1970. San Diego, Calif.: San Diego State College, September 1970. ED 044727

Lipton, Gladys C., editor. "FLES: Projections into the Future. A report by the FLES Committee of the American Association of Teachers of French." Presented November 29, 1968, Boston. New York: Modern Language Association Materials Center, 1969. ED 052644

Littlejohn, Joseph E. "A Handbook for Teacher and Aides of the Choctaw Bilingual Education Program." Durant, Okla.: Southeastern State College, August 1971. ED 054902

Lopez, Thomas F. "Staff Development of Bilingual Programs." Master's thesis submitted to Sacramento State College, California, June 1970. ED 044233

Lusty, Beverly L., and Wood, Barbara Sundene. "Effects of an NDEA Institute Upon Attitudes of Inner-City Elementary Teachers." *Spanish Teacher* 18: 217-22; September 1969.

Majer, Kenneth S. "Comtemporary Comment on Changing Teacher Education." Bloomington: Indiana University, 1973. ED 082124

MacDiarmid, Jim. "The Student in a Bilingual Classroom." Northern Cross-Cultural Education Symposium, Yupik, May 1974. ED 094921

Malkoc, Anna Maria, compiler. "A TESOL Bibliography: Abstracts of ERIC Publications and Research Reports, 1969-1970." Washington, D.C.: Center for Applied Linguistics, 1971. ED 047295

Manpower. "Driving Ambition Pays Off in Jobs." *Manpower* 3: 28-30; April 1971.

Marchwardt, Albert H. "The Relationship Between TESOL and the Center for Applied Linguistics." Paper presented at the Sixth Annual TESOL Convention, Washington, D.C., February 1972. ED 064997

Martinson, Ruth, and Ruthmeyer, Robert. "A Report on Research and Teacher Education Projects for Disadvantaged Children. Description and Present Status of Projects, 1965-1966." Sacramento: California State Department of Education, 1967. ED 022814

Mathieson, Moira B. "A Brief Bibliography on Teacher Education and American Indians." Washington, D.C.: ERIC Clearinghouse on Teacher Education, 1974. ED 090146

Mazon, Manuel Reyes, and Arciniega, Tomas A. "Competency-Based Education and the Culturally Different: A Role of Hope, or More of the Same?" (Preliminary draft.) Washington, D.C.: American Association of Colleges for Teacher Education, 1974. ED 092522

McCahon, David. "Evaluation of Pittsburgh Teacher Corps Pre-Service Program—Fourth Cycle." Pittsburgh, Pa.: School of Education, University of Pittsburgh, 1969. ED 047001

McClafferty, James, and others. "Foreign Language Innovative Curricula Studies. End of Grant Period Report. Title III, ESEA, 1968-1969." Ann Arbor, Mich.: Ann Arbor Public Schools, 1969. ED 035327

McMagh, P. "The Teaching of English as a Second Language in Primary Schools in the Cape Province." Pretoria: English Academy of Southern Africa, 1967. ED 027542

Michel, Joseph. "The Preparation of the Teacher for Bilingual Education." Speech presented at Edinboro State College, Pennsylvania, September 1972. ED 063830

Miller, James O. "An Educational Imperative and Its Fallout Implications." Paper presented to President's Committee on Mental Retardation Conference, Warrenton, Va., August 10-12, 1969. ED 034590

Miller, Louise. "A Need for a Competency Based Teacher Education for Native Americans. Position Paper," 1974. ED 091387

Muchley, Robert L. "After Childhood, Then What? An Overview of Ethnic Language Retention (ELRET) Programs in the United States." Quebec: International Center on Bilingualism, Leval University, November 1971. ED 061808

Munoz, Olivia. "La Ensenanza del Espanol ante la Inquieta Sociedad (The Study of Spanish in A Period of Unrest)." *Hispania* 54: 34-38; March 1971.

Natalicio, Diana S., and William, Frederick. "Oral Language Assessment." Paper presented at the annual meeting of the American Educational Research Association, Chicago, April 1972. ED 063845

National Council of Teachers of English, Task Force on Teaching English to the Disadvantaged. "Language Programs for the Disadvantaged." Champaign, Ill.: the Council, 1965. ED 036506

National Education Association. "Teaching the Rural Disadvantaged: Preliminary Bibliography." Washington, D.C.: Department of Rural Education, National Education Association, March 1968. ED 020062

National Science Teachers Association. "Association for the Education of Teachers of Science, Compilation of Papers and Reports from Sessions Held in Conjunction with the Convention of the National Science Teachers Association (New York City, April 1-2, 1966)." Washington, D.C.: the Association, 1966. ED 017471

Newell, John, and others. "Migrant Early Childhood Education Program in Hardee County, Florida: An Evaluation." Gainesville, Fla.: Institute for Development of Human Resources, August 1971. ED 060960

Newman, Laurence. "Bilingual Education." *Deaf American* 25: 12-13; May 1973.

New York City Board of Education, Office of Bilingual Education. "Building Bridges to Better Bilingual Education." Brooklyn: the Board, 1973. ED 081273

Nimnicht, Glen P., and others. "A Report on the Evaluation of the Parent/Child Toy-Lending Library Program." Berkeley, Calif.: Far West Laboratory for Educational Research and Development, August 1971. ED 069655

Oettle, Sylvia. "Language Arts Programs for Disadvantaged Children in Secondary Schools." Newark: New Jersey Association of Teachers of English, April 1969. ED 043605

Ohannessian, Sirarpi, and others. "Conference on Navajo Orthography." Washington, D.C.: English for Speakers of Other Languages Program, Center for Applied Linguistics, June 1969. ED 044668

"Operation Probe: Cooperative Urban Teacher Education." Kansas City, Mo.: Association for Student Teaching, Midcontinent Regional Educational Laboratory, September 1968. ED 028965

Oregon State University. "Second Cycle Teacher Corps Program. Final Report." Corvallis: the University, 1969. ED 042704

Pablano, Ralph. "Ghosts in the Barrio: Issues in Bilingual Bicultural Education." San Rafael, Calif.: Leswing Press, 1973. ED 085128

Palmer, Judith A. "Preschool Education Pros and Cons: A Survey of 'Pre-School' Education with Emphasis on Research Past, Present, and Future." Toronto, Ont.: Board of Education, April 1966. ED 016525

Perales, Alonso M., and others. "Training Teachers for Bilingual Bicultural Education." *Hispania* 56: 762-66; October 1973.

Pfeiffer, Anita. "The Role of TESOL in Bilingual Education for the Navajo Child," March 1969. ED 028447

Philadelphia Public Schools. "Ford Projections—The Ford Foundation Project Schools Newsletter." Philadelphia: the Schools, May 1962. ED 001021

Politzer, Robert L., and Diana E. Bartley. "Practice-Centered Teacher Training: Standard English is a Second Dialect." *Modern Language Journal* 53: 565; December 1969.

Porter, M. Rosemonde. "Curriculum Improvement Program in English Language Skills for Schools of the Trust Territory of the Pacific Islands. Final Report." Honolulu: College of Education, University of Hawaii, June 1969. ED 033338

Purvis, N. M. "Northwest Territories Teacher Education Program." *Elements: Translating Theory into Practice* 3: 5-6; March 1972.

Ramirez, Manuel III. "Potential Contributions by the Behavioral Sciences to Effective Preparation Programs for Teachers of Mexican-American Children." Paper prepared for the Conference on Teacher Education for Mexican Americans, New Mexico State University, February 13-15, 1969. ED 025370

Redbird-Salam, Helen Marie, and Salam, Leroy B. "Cultural Conflict in the Classroom." *Social Education* 36: 513-19; May 1972.

Richburg, James R., and Rice, M. J. "Accountability in Minority Teacher Training: The University of Georgia Indian Teacher Training Program." Paper presented at the College and Faculty Association Section of the annual meeting of the National Council for the Social Studies, Boston, November 21, 1972. ED 076466

Rippey, Robert M. "Report of an Urban Education Reform Experiment: Problems and Promises. Section II: Project Evaluation. Supplement to the Final Report of the 5th Cycle Teacher Corps Project." Chicago: University of Illinois, 1972. ED 087746

Resource Management Corporation. "Full-Scale Implementation of a Process Evaluation System for Programs of the National Center for the Improvement of Educational Systems. Vol. 1: Summary." Bethesda, Md.: Resource Management Corporation, November 1972. ED 067522

Rodriguez, Armando. "Bilingual Education—A Look Ahead," 1969. ED 030505

————. "Urban Education and the Mexican-American." Speech given at Ford Foundation Leadership Seminar, Albuquerque, August 23, 1968. ED 030510

Rodriguez, Louis P. "Preparing Teachers for the Spanish-Speaking." *National Elementary Principal* 50: 50-52; November 1970.

Rowe, John L. "Challenges Ahead for Teacher Education." *American Vocational Journal* 45: 26-29; February 1970.

Rubeck, Robert F., and others. "A Guide for Urban-Teacher Development. Final Report." Columbus, Ohio; Battelle Memorial Institute, November 1970. ED 046886

Ruong, Israel. "Lapp Schools, Teacher Education and Transcultural Studies." Speech prepared for the International Conference on Cross-Cultural Education, Montreal, August 1969. ED 092277

Sagness, Richard Lee. "A Study of Selected Outcomes of a Science Pre-Service Teacher Education Project Emphasizing Early Involvement in Schools of Contrasting Environmental Settings." Columbus: Ohio State University, 1970. ED 052994

Sandstrom, Roy H., editor. "Clash of Cultures: A Report of the Institute on the American Indian Student in Higher Education, July 10-28, 1972." Canton, N.Y.: St. Lawrence University, 1972. ED 085147

San Francisco Unified School District. "Early Childhood and School-Age Intensive Education Program: Evaluation of the ESEA Compensatory Program of the San Francisco Unified School District, 1968-1969. Evaluation Report." San Francisco: the District, January 1970. ED 041066

Saunders, Jack O. L. "The Blueprint Potentials of the Cooperative Teacher Education Preparation; Utilizing the Talented Mexican American." Paper prepared for the Conference on Teacher Education for Mexican Americans, New Mexico State University, Las Cruces, February 13-15, 1969. ED 025372

Saville-Troike, Muriel. "TESOL Today: The Need for New Directions," October 1974. ED 096833

Schmitt, Henry E., "Teacher Education for the Culturally Different. Appendix C of a Final Report." Columbus: Center for Vocational and Technical Education, Ohio State University, January 31, 1973. ED 072207

————. "Teacher Preparation for the Culturally Different. Does the Profession Believe the Cause Is Worth the Effort?" *Agricultural Education Magazine* 43: 282-83; May 1971.

Schoenbeck, Paul H. "Motivation: By Whom—For What?" Paper presented at the National Reading Conference, St. Petersburg, Florida, December 3-5, 1970. ED 047915

Schwartz, Sheila, editor. *Teaching the Humanities: Selected Readings.* New York: Macmillan Co., 1970. ED 041904

Schweitzer, Paul, and others. "Evaluation of Decentralized ESEA Title I Programs, District 23, New York City Board of Education, 1970-1971 School Year." Bronx: Fordham University Institute for Research and Evaluation, 1971. ED 060150

Sekaquaptewa, Eugene. "Desirable (Innovative) Training Programs for the Teachers of Indians. A Position Paper." Albuquerque: Southwestern Cooperative Educational Laboratory, April 1970. ED 057958

"Seminar on the Training of Teachers, by the Interdisciplinary System, To Use This System in School (Bouake, Ivory Coast, March 24-April 4, 1970). Final Report." Paris: United Nations Educational, Scientific, and Cultural Organization, 1970. ED 049174

Short, Evelyn H. "Teacher Corps at New Mexico State University. Final Narrative Report: Cycle II." Las Cruces: New Mexico State University, 1969. ED 042702

Simon, Roger I., and others. "IMPACTE: A Descriptive Report and Evaluation of the First 18 Months (Indian and Metis Project for Careers Through Teacher Education)." Ottawa, Ont.: Department of Indian Affairs and Northern Development, 1973. ED 097145

Slager, William, and Madsen, Betty M., editors. "Language in American Indian Education." A Newsletter of the Office of Education Programs. Albuquerque: Bureau of Indian Affairs, U.S. Department of the Interior, 1971. ED 061788

Smith, Anne M. "Indian Education in New Mexico." Albuquerque: Division of Government Research, University of New Mexico, July 1968. ED 025345

Soriano, Jesse M., and McClafferty, Jones. "Spanish Speakers of the Midwest: They Are Americans Too." *Foreign Language Annual* 2: 316-24; March 1969.

Spolsky, Bernard, editor. "Advances in Navajo Bilingual Education 1969-72." Navajo Reading Study Progress Report No. 20. Albuquerque: University of New Mexico, 1972. ED 069461

_____. "The Navajo Reading Study: An Illustration of the Scope and Nature of Educational Linguistics." Paper presented at the Third International Congress of Applied Linguistics, Copenhagen, August 1972. ED 077267

Squire, James R., and others. "Source Book on English Institutes for Elementary Teachers." Champaign, Ill.: Modern Language Association of America and National Council of Teachers of English, 1965. ED 037430

Stent, Madelon D.; Hazard, William; and Rivlin, Harry, editors. *Cultural Pluralism in Education: A Mandate for Change.* New York: Appleton-Century-Crofts, 1973. ED 086782

Strain, Jeris E. "English Language Instruction in Iran." Oswego: New York State English Council, April 1971. ED 054661

Stryker, David, editor. "Educating the Teacher of English: Selected Addresses Delivered at the Conference on English Education." Champaign, Ill.: National Council of Teachers of English, 1965. ED 070102

_____. "New Trends in English Education: Selected Addresses Delivered at the Conference on English Education (Fourth, Carnegie Institute of Technology, March 31-April 2, 1966)." Champaign, Ill.: National Council of Teachers of English, 1966. ED 070101

Student National Education Association. "New Teachers: New Education." Student Impact Occasional Paper. Washington, D.C.: the Association, May 1970. ED 042733

Sullivan, John J. "EPDA-COP Students Receive Degrees." *Journal of American Indian Education* 14: 13-15; October 1974.

Taschow, Horst G. "A Comparative Study of Diagnosis and Therapy in Children with Reading Deficiencies in the German and English Language." Paper presented at the International Reading Association World Congress on Reading, Vienna, August 1974. ED 098550

Theimer, William C. Jr., editor. "Career Opportunity Programs. Improving Opportunities for Success in Education." Stockton: California Laboratory of Educational Research, University of the Pacific, April 1971. ED 055040

Trevino, Robert E. "Is Bilingual Education Shortchanging the Chicano?" Paper prepared for a Symposium on the Education of Mexican Americans, Society for Applied Anthropology Meeting, Tucson, April 1973. ED 077617

Trinity College. "The Bilingual-Bicultural Education Program of the Institute of American Studies." Washington, D.C.: the College, 1972. ED 079275

Troike, Rudolph C. "Statement on Linguistic Concerns in Bilingual Education." Paper presented to the National Advisory Committee on the Education of Bilingual Children, Washington, D.C., January 1974. ED 093176

Ulibarri, Horacio. "Attitudinal Characteristics of Migrant Farm Workers. First Papers on Migrancy and Rural Poverty: An Introduction to the Education of Mexican Americans in Rural Areas." Los Angeles: School of Education, University of Southern California, 1968. ED 026172

University of Arizona. "The Cultural Literacy Laboratory: A New Dimension in Multicultural Teacher Education." Tucson: the University, 1973. ED 087698

University of California. "Workpapers: Teaching English as a Second Language, Vol. V." Los Angeles: the University, June 1971. ED 056556

University of Southern California. "Teacher Corps—Urban Cycle II, Final Program Report." Los Angeles: the University, 1969. ED 042689

University of Texas. "Proposed Undergraduate Program for Compensatory Bilingual-Bidialectal Education." Austin: College of Education, University of Texas, April 1970. ED 037718

University of Toledo. "Toledo Teacher Corps: An Undergraduate Program for the Development of Teachers for the Inner City." Toledo, Ohio: College of Education, the University, 1969. ED 042690

U.S. Department of Health, Education, and Welfare, Office of Education. "Mexican American Education: Special Report." Washington, D.C.: Mexican American Affairs Unit, Office of Education, March 1968. ED 023510

U.S. Department of the Interior, Bureau of Indian Affairs. "Indian Education: Steps to Progress in the 70's." Washington, D.C.: the Bureau, 1973. ED 081537

Valencia, Atilano A. "The Effects of a College Teacher Training Project with Emphases on Mexican American Cultural Characteristics. An Evaluation Report." Sacramento, Calif.: Sacramento State College, September 1970. ED 045267

_____. "Identification and Assessment of Ongoing Educational and Community Programs for Spanish Speaking People." A report submitted to the Southwest Council of La Raza, Phoenix, Arizona, March 1969. ED 028013

Van Meter, and Barba, Alma, editors. "Regional Conference on Teacher Education for Mexican-Americans. Conference Proceedings." Papers prepared for the Conference on Teacher Education for Mexican Americans, New Mexico State University, February 13-15, 1969. ED 027444

Walsh, Sister Marie Andre. "Preparing Teachers for Bilingual Schools." Paper presented at the North American French Bilingual Conference, Lafayette, Louisiana, 1972. ED 071486

Washington, Bennetta B. "Cardozo Project in Urban Teaching: A Pilot Project in Curriculum Development Utilizing Returned Peace Corps Volunteers in an Urban High School. Interim Report." Washington, D.C.: District of Columbia Public Schools, January 1964. ED 001653

Watson, Guy A. "Training for Cross-Cultural Teaching." *Audio-Visual Instructor* 14: 50-54; January 1969

Wilder, Mary Roberts. "An Evaluation of the Pre-Service and In-Service Academic Preparation in English for Teachers of Disadvantaged Students in Selected Colleges in the State of Georgia." Doctoral dissertation. Tallahassee: Florida State University, 1970. (Unpublished) ED 056037

Wilson, Herbert B. "Quality Education in a Multicultural Classroom." *Childhood Education* 50: 153-56; January 1974

Wilson, Roger. "Teacher Corps: A Model for Training Teachers. Position Paper." Paper presented at the Native American Teacher Corps Conference, Denver, Colorado, April 26-29, 1973. ED 075134

Womack, Thurston. "Preparing Teachers for TESOL—Where We've Been, Where We Are, and Maybe Where We Should Be Going." Paper presented at the Fifth Annual TESOL Convention, New Orleans, March 6, 1971. ED 051726

Zintz, Miles V.; Ulibarri, Marie L.; and Gonzales, Dolores. "The Implications of Bilingual Education for Developing Multicultural Sensitivity Through Teacher Education." Washington, D.C.: ERIC Clearinghouse on Teacher Education, September 1971. ED 054071